May '18

Dear Traci —

Thanks you all the

you do to liben

lines of so many.

Love,

Brad Wilcox

CONVERTED

unto the Lord

CONTENTS

The Grandeur of God
Matthew O. Richardson 119

Stay on the Bus: Experiencing the Power of Jesus Christ
Deeply and Regularly
Brad Wilcox 129

Fighting the Fear That We Aren't Good Enough
Kathy E. Zeyer 137

Sharing the Knowledge of a Savior
Elder Gary E. Stevenson 150

Notes 161

Contributors 167

EYES TO SEE, DISCIPLINE TO CREATE, GLUE TO BIND–CONVERTED UNTO THE LORD

Sharon Eubank

A few months ago, I went to an Asian café in town for lunch. The friendly guy behind the counter said: "Have you ever been here before?" And I confessed no. "Okay, pick your starch, your protein, and your sauce." I had never thought of lunch that way before and it struck me that there were almost endless combinations made from these three basic building blocks for a meal:

- Pasta, meatballs, and marinara
- Rice, chicken, sweet and sour
- Spaetzle, beef, and stroganoff
- Tortillas, carne asada, and salsa
- Brown rice, tofu, and curry
- Rye, pastrami, and mustard
- Potatoes, steak, and A.1.
- Biscuits, ham, and gravy
- Angel hair pasta, scallops, cream
- Waffles, bacon, and syrup

I've thought about this a lot since that day. What would be the main building blocks of conversion? What are the basic experiences we all have that combine into an endless variety?

BUILDING BLOCKS OF TRUE CONVERSION

I have come to believe there are three basic ingredients to the feast of each person's conversion. We all have experiences with these key ingredients but each has such a different look and taste that it's not always easy to compare our conversions. There is no one conversion. It's the Atonement that gives us the multiple chances we need to repent and to combine these three ingredients into a satisfying feast of true conversion.

The first ingredient is learning to see beyond the mortal limits of time and space.

On earth we are bound by limits:

- During the seventy to ninety years of an average life, we can only experience a fraction of the stream of time. It's very difficult to look forward or backward to see the big picture.
- Our memory is very poor. We forget almost everything unless we write it down.
- Frailty, illness, energy, disease, and death limit us physically, mentally, and emotionally.
- Pride, conflict, and the quest for power are constantly disrupting our attempts to come together and accomplish something as a group.
- We cannot prove the truth to others; they must find it for themselves.

Transcending the limits of mortal time and space is the power to see "things as they really are" (Jacob 4:13), not how they look on the earth. One person able to do it was the brother of Jared. He was able to pierce the veil and see the bodily form Jesus would take later on earth (see Ether 3:6–13). Another to do it was Sarah, who looked beyond a suffocating personal grief and let her only beloved son walk out on a journey with his father, Abraham (see Genesis 22). Another name for this ability to see beyond right now is *faith*.

What would it mean for you and me in the twenty-first century to think beyond mortal limits? It means the fashions of the day, the opinions on Twitter, the handicaps and barriers of this brief mortal life are just that—brief. They don't last. We women are called to focus on what lasts. From the very beginning, Eve took a really long look through the veil. What is mortal life for? To hang around in the beautiful garden? She realized that to have birth there had to be death. In order for Eve and Adam to multiply and replenish the earth, she had to choose to eat the fruit. To open the door for all of us to come into mortality, she had to trigger the fall. She sacrificed a Garden of Eden kind of life in order to bring us all through the veil. She became the mother of all living. Her ultimate testimony to all her children is: "Were it not for our transgression we never should have known good and evil, and the joy of our redemption, and the eternal life which God giveth unto all the obedient" (Moses 5:11). She could do it because she put her complete confidence in Jesus Christ. She and Adam had the faith that Jesus would accomplish His Atoning work. Jesus promised to compensate for the fall of Adam and Eve. And He did. His Atonement removes the barriers of sin, injustice, mistakes, ignorance, and pain at the hands of others so that if we have faith and keep covenants with Him, we will transcend or overcome the limits of this fallen world. Every challenge we encounter in life will help us learn to use revelation, or eyes of faith, to look past the realities of this world into the better world.

I want to share three examples of women who used their eyes of faith to look beyond present pain and circumstance.

I read recently a BBC survey where 31 percent of Christians polled believed in the literal resurrection of Jesus.[1] That means 69 percent of Christians in that poll do not believe Jesus actually rose from the dead in a physical form. We just celebrated Easter. I like to imagine early in the morning before dawn Jesus as a spirit coming into the tomb before He was resurrected. The grave clothes would have to be unwound from the body before He could enter it. In John 20 it describes how the napkin that had been around his head was folded and laid on one side and the clothing on the other (see John 20:7). When the body was ready for Him, I imagine Jesus's spirit entered it. Was there light or sound at the resurrection? I don't know. But I do know that when the heavy stone was rolled away and Jesus walked out of the grave, "the firstfruits of them that slept" (1 Corinthians 15:20), the limits of death and hell stopped having power on this earth. There was now a living, physical example of those scriptural promises that the dead should rise again. Of course, it was hard to mentally grasp. Mary Magdalene, full of grief in the garden, couldn't believe it at first, but when Jesus spoke her name and she reached out to embrace Him, she knew Him. She knew what resurrection meant (see John 20:11–18). Mary Magdalene was the first mortal witness to testify: He is risen (see Matthew 28:7).

If we as Christians don't believe that Jesus is resurrected and brings resurrection to us all, then we live in a dead world. Things

CONVERTED
unto the Lord

TALKS FROM THE 2017
BYU WOMEN'S CONFERENCE

DESERET
BOOK

SALT LAKE CITY, UTAH

Printing of the First Book of Mormon, page 153, courtesy Gary E. Smith.
Family photo, page 157, courtesy Gary E. Stevenson.

Library of Congress Cataloging-in-Publication Data

Names: Women's Conference (2017 : Brigham Young University), author.
Title: Converted unto the Lord : talks from the 2017 BYU Women's Conference.
Description: Salt Lake City, Utah : Deseret Book, [2018] | Includes bibliographical references.
Identifiers: LCCN 2017046130 | ISBN 9781629724386 (hardbound : alk. paper)
Subjects: LCSH: Mormon women—Conduct of life—Congresses. | Mormon women—Religious life—Congresses. | The Church of Jesus Christ of Latter-day Saints—Doctrines—Congresses. | Mormon Church—Doctrines—Congresses.
Classification: LCC BX8656 .W6 2017b | DDC 248.8/43088289332—dc23
LC record available at https://lccn.loc.gov/2017046130

Printed in the United States of America
Edwards Brothers Malloy, Ann Arbor, MI

10   9   8   7   6   5   4   3   2   1

die and don't revive. Dead children, dead dreams, dead relationships. Mary is the first in a cloud of witnesses that the death which defines our time in mortality and feels so permanent is really only temporary. Jesus Christ was resurrected. We, too, will be resurrected. The sureness of resurrection makes a very big difference to me in the way I view the world and the things I choose to do. Women like us who have made covenants must join Mary Magdalene as witnesses. There is life after death, and the kind of life we gain after death depends on our choices now.

The second example is of three women who made a painful choice but had the hope that it wasn't a final choice. It is the story of the daughters of Onitah told in Abraham 1.

In the land of Chaldeans (modern-day Baghdad), the people had turned from righteousness to idolatry because of the false teachings of the Egyptians (see Abraham 1:5–8). The priest of Pharaoh had built an altar in the land of Chaldea and he was sacrificing men, women, and children to the sun god, Shagreel (see Abraham 1:9).

Abraham 1:11 reads: "Now, this priest had offered upon this altar three virgins at one time, who were the daughters of Onitah, one of the royal descent directly from the loins of Ham. These virgins were offered up because of their virtue; they would not bow down to worship gods of wood or of stone, therefore they were killed upon this altar, and it was done after the manner of the Egyptians."

These three young women's choice to stand as a witness was their final act in mortal life but that decision opened up an eternal world of promise to them. Of these three virgins, Neal A. Maxwell said: "Matching [Shadrach, Meshach, and Abed-nego] are three young women whose names we do not have. They appear in the Book of Abraham, remarkable young women about whom I am anxious to know more. They were sacrificed upon the altar because 'they would not bow down to worship [an idol] of wood or stone.' Someday the faithful will get to meet them."[2]

For the last example, let me introduce you to Reyna Aburto. She is a woman who truly knows how to see what really matters. She and I have really only known each other a few weeks, but we have become trusted friends. This is her story:

"A terrible earthquake hit Nicaragua just after midnight on December 23, 1972.[3] My house collapsed in a few seconds. I was saved because a piece of furniture behind me protected me with a space to breathe. My mother and some neighbors helped me out. It was pitch dark. I remember just sitting across the street and looking at where the house used to be. It felt like a nightmare. I didn't think it was real. Being only nine years old I was thinking: Where will we live now? What clothes will I wear? It felt like everything stopped and I didn't know what would come next. But we received so much help from neighbors, family members, even strangers. Gradually life started to make sense again. We eventually had another house, another table, another bed, another place to live. I learned not to be attached to material things but instead to focus on what really matters.

"10,000 people died in the earthquake that night. My ten-year-old brother sleeping on a bed next to me was killed. He and I were close. It didn't feel real that he was gone. I was in shock for months. Years later when I was a teenager I had a kind of fantasy. I was obsessed with the idea that my brother would knock on our front door and tell us that he had just been away somewhere, that he wasn't really dead. I can remember staring at the front door and wanting it to happen. At some level I knew it was silly but I wanted so much to see him again.

"Then four years ago, I was standing at my kitchen sink in Orem washing the dishes. It was Eastertime and I was thinking of the resurrection for some reason. I thought of my brother and suddenly a feeling came over me. I got it. It wasn't silly. That vivid obsession I had about seeing him at the door was really a revelation from the Holy Ghost, even though I was too young to understand it and not a member of the Church. It was telling me that he really is somewhere. He will be resurrected and I am going to see him again."[4]

Reyna relates that her physical world as a young girl was full of uncertainty, insecurity, shock, and sorrow, but the Lord taught her as a teenager through a vivid daydream and the whisperings of the Holy Ghost about the reality that exists beyond this mortal world.

President J. Reuben Clark Jr. said something very powerful about this ability to see beyond what is visible to our physical eyes as we exercise faith. He said: "As I think about faith, this principle of power, I am obliged to believe that it is an intelligent force. Of what kind I do not know. But it is superior to and overrules all other forces of which we know. . . . [We] have had this great power given unto us . . . What are we doing about it? . . . If you but live the Gospel, . . . you may invoke the power which is within you."[5]

Consider the example of Eve, or the daughters of Onitah, Mary Magdalene, or Reyna Aburto. Then take a long look into eternity, into what really matters. Hold fast to the vision of what you see that is true. The Lord told Emma Smith that her role and the role of all of us was to "lay aside the things of this world, and seek for the things of a better" (Doctrine and Covenants 25:10). If you exercise the power of your faith then the stark realities of this life—the restrictions, the abuses, the things that are unfair, the barriers—only exist temporarily. And you are eternal. The priesthood power that comes to you by keeping your covenants in faith is also eternal and propels you continually past the limits of now.

But what if you are blinded by what is going on in your life? What if you can't find the faith to see beyond the stifling things that are happening to you right now? We've all felt that way too.

About a year ago I had eye surgery so that one of my eyes would see far away and the other one close up. The surgeon warned me that it would take weeks for my brain to separate which picture from which eye it was looking at and adjust. After the surgery, I knew I had made a severe mistake. My vision was like looking at everything underwater. I couldn't read. My focus jumped back and forth between the eyes. I had a monster head-ache. I had been prescribed eye drops to use every two hours, but I was easily distracted and couldn't remember to use them. When I went back to the doctor, I was frustrated and complained that my vision wasn't getting any better. "Are you using the eye drops faithfully?" I wanted to say yes. But the real answer was no. "The eye drops are the key to your new vision." Fine. So I started to use them. I kept them in my pocket and in the car and at work and on my bedtable. They became a part of my daily routine. Slowly over several weeks my eyesight began to improve. The more I used the drops, the better I could see. After six weeks, my vision had improved to be vastly better than before the surgery. I was so happy. What made the difference? The skill of the surgeon and the laser technology were both important, but it was my remembering the simple eye drops that only took a small amount of time every day that allowed everything else to work together so that I could see.

If we want to develop the faith to see in new ways, beyond this life, then small drops are the key to our new vision. What are the drops? Acting on what you know. If we get distracted and don't act on the things we know, our eyesight starts to dim and get wavy. We get a monster spiritual headache. When we act regularly on our testimonies, our vision slowly improves until we are seeing things we never had in the past.

Elder David A. Bednar taught: "Knowing that the gospel is true is the essence of a testimony. Consistently being true to the gospel is the essence of conversion. We should know the gospel is true and be true to the gospel."[6]

So take a long look through the veil and focus on things that really matter. What will we keep with us on the other side of that veil? Relationships, covenants, knowledge, testimony, experiences, repentance, mercy, service. Then, don't just know them, DO them. That is the secret to the recipe for being converted to the Lord.

To summarize this first ingredient of true conversion: **The ability of women to see beyond the limits of mortal time and space is called *faith*.**

The barriers of this world aren't real or permanent. Priesthood power transcends mortal limits. Experiences with faith lead to testimony. Acting on testimony brings conversion. Women can be seers for their own lives. Faith in Jesus Christ is the foundation of this building block.

The second ingredient of true conversion is about using the body as an instrument of power, order, and creation.

Now I'll tell you a story about grief. When I was thirteen years old, my Beehive teacher told the nine of us in the class that, according to statistics, at least one of us in the circle wouldn't get married. I looked around the group and thought to myself, "Well, of course it won't be me." I had plans to be married and all the things I would teach my children, how I would share my favorite books with them, how I would keep traditions for our holidays, how I would make them peanut butter sandwiches and wash the jam off their cheeks before putting them down to sleep. How they would roll their eyes at my quirky mom jokes, how I would be the world's coolest grandma. But surprisingly to me, I haven't ended up marrying in this life, and I don't have my children with me right now. This was a physical grief I could hardly bear for many years. Thirteen years ago, on a Sunday in May, I walked out of my house to get into the car to go to church, and I noticed that during the night the big maple trees had sent out all their helicopter seed pods into the grass. There was something about this image of the mother trees sending out thousands of their children into the world that stopped my heart. I can't explain it. The grief was so terrible that I couldn't cry or even speak. I felt sterile and wasted and truly damned.

It is part of our spiritual birthright to be creators. President Dieter F. Uchtdorf expressed it famously: "The desire to create is one of the deepest yearnings of the human soul. No matter our talents, education, backgrounds, or abilities, we each have an inherent wish to create something that did not exist before.

"Everyone can create. You don't need money, position, or influence in order to create something of substance or beauty.

"Creation brings deep satisfaction and fulfillment. . . .

"Remember that you are spirit daughters of the most creative Being in the universe. . . .

"The more you trust and rely upon the Spirit, the greater your capacity to create. That is your opportunity in this life and your destiny in the life to come. Sisters, trust and rely on the Spirit. As you take the normal opportunities of your daily life and create something of beauty and helpfulness, you improve not only the world around you but also the world within you."[7]

In one of the highest expressions of creation, men and women create in tandem. Marriage is the process of two equal beings coming together to become a whole unit. Welded or sealed together by priesthood authority they become authorized to combine and create life. Our bodies are made for creation but only under certain circumstances and parameters. A creation "key" we call "being sealed for time and eternity" has to be turned in order for us to be authorized to create life. It's true we can act without authorization, but if we do and don't repent, we lose the ability to keep our creations with us after this life.

Family comes from the union of creators under law. Eternal family results from using the powerful instrument of the body in a specific and ordained way with discipline, covenants, patience, faith, hard work, great love, sacrifice, consecration, chastity, obedience, and law. When creation occurs in this way, our creations stay bonded to us forever.

Now creation isn't only about children, as President Uchtdorf says. "We each have an inherent wish to create something that did not exist before."[8] And there are many ways for women to multiply, replenish, and create in the world.

Elder M. Russell Ballard said: "There is nothing in this world as personal . . . or as life changing as the influence of a righteous woman. . . . *All* women have within their divine nature both the inherent talent and the stewardship to mother."[9]

In the story I told you about the maple seed pods, I didn't understand this principle well. At least not well enough to be converted to it. On a very powerful emotional level, I felt I had been stopped from being a creator. I wasn't able to use my eyes to look beyond the barriers of this life. Do you know what helped me get past this heavy grief . . . honestly? Relief Society. I was around women who acknowledged emotionally that I am still a creator. Not having my husband and children with me at this time is temporary. I have been a being with creative gifts for millennia. There are laws on this earth that help me discipline my body and my will so I can create even more powerfully in the future. Every day I am creating influence, compassion, love, and grace that did not previously exist.

In addition to using our bodies as instruments of power and discipline to receive life through the veil, we also have the chance to give life back through the veil. We speak often of women's roles in birth, but we do not as often speak of their roles in death. Let me give an example very personal to me.

Last November, a woman who was like a sister to me—a thirty-eight-year-old wife and mother of two girls—was in the last throes of her fight with lung cancer. I watched as her sisters surrounded the bed in the UCLA medical center. They held her hands, they rubbed her feet, they kept her warm, they fed her ice, they told her jokes. She was afraid to die, and they knew that. At the very last, they held her in their arms until she passed from the room, telling her it was okay to go and that they would take care of her children. These women acted in godly perfection. They are now creating a family that will have to stretch out of the traditional shape for the needs it now faces. In a very tangible way they share in the creation of childhood for two girls, along with the mother and father who gave them life.

Joseph Smith told the Relief Society in 1842 that because they were now organized after a priesthood pattern: "You are now placed in a situation where you can act according to those sympathies which God has planted in your [hearts]. . . . If you live up to your privilege, the angels cannot be restrained from being your associates."[10]

The sisters of my friend are counting on that promise of angels to help them in their divine work on behalf of their little sister who is gone.

There is going to be a lot of opposition to our attempts at using our bodies as instruments of order and creation. Having a body is extremely powerful, and there are potent forces arrayed to try to destroy what the body can do. This is a war Jesus Christ perfectly understands, and He can heal us from our battle scars and restore our body's strength that earlier may have been misspent. Honest repentance can recover what was lost.

To summarize this second ingredient of true conversion, we are on earth to: **Use our bodies as instruments of power, order, and creation** that fully become "operational" under the discipline of covenants. All women are creators. The mastery of understanding the law, acting within the law, and repenting when we cross outside the law is a large part of true conversion. Family is the result of this building block of conversion.

The third and final ingredient of conversion is to practice unity and love.

The Savior said to Peter: "Simon, Simon, behold, Satan hath desired to . . . sift you as wheat: But I have prayed for thee, that thy faith fail not: and when thou art converted, strengthen thy brethren" (Luke 22:31–32).

Strengthening others is evidence of our conversion to the Lord. It is the sauce that gives flavor to the rest of the meal. The women who do this well, do it so masterfully that it is almost invisible. Let me tell you about meeting Jeri Cook.

Ten years ago, I was on my first assignment to the Middle East. I was nervous. The first event of the trip was a missionary couple's conference in Amman, Jordan. I arrived a day early, thinking I would prepare for the conference. Instead, I ended up working in Sister Jeri Cook's white, well-used kitchen and talking with her while we cooked. When I offered to help, she first had me make a Betty Crocker cake with Arabic instructions, and when that was cooling, she had me chop vegetables, fry hamburger, and make two big pots of soup.

With the two of us working, there was plenty of time to chat about how she and her husband were married when they were both eighteen; how they got the courage to leave Pleasant Grove, Utah, as a young, very poor couple and take a job in Saudi Arabia; and how she had loved her mission in Jordan. I asked about her family from the pictures on the fridge, and she talked about each one with tremendous pride. Whenever a new couple arrived for the conference, Sister Cook would stop what she was doing and throw her arms around them. They were frazzled from irritating border crossings and heavy traffic, and she would welcome them inside.

Meanwhile, her husband, Elder Cook, was busy arranging other details: figuring out the logistics to pick up Elder Holland at the airport, then on the phone confirming the next day's appointments at the Ministry of Health, and haggling with the heating oil guy. If someone asked which of the Cooks was more productive that day on their mission—how can that possibly be answered?

But that evening, the five couples sat around the large dining room table and shared stories over soup and bread, juice and cake. It was a homey meal in a warm setting and the camaraderie flowed in a way people would remember fondly after their missions were over. The couples were tired and used up from their difficult assignments. I was nervous about a new position I didn't know how to fill. I realized it was Sister Cook's gentle ministry which laid the foundation for the rest and faith and happiness we all felt that night.

We women are often like Jeri Cook. We throw our arms around the people who come and go. We have a refrigerator door full of pictures of people we love. We take a younger woman under our wing and involve her with whatever we are doing while we talk. I have no doubt each one of us would move the earth for the people in those photos on our kitchen walls. But so often we don't want to scare them with our power to bless and heal, so we move the world in increments of soup and cake. They may never even recognize the universe has been realigned for their good. It may be that our mother does glorious things right in front of us every day so often that she blinds us with commonness. Maybe she serves the whole world soup and cake every night.

I wish I had a fancy name for it, but women are called to be glue. They create the bonds of unity and kindness. You see it in matriarchs who are the center of things. They reach out and include people, they find meaningful things for each person to do, they make sure the right things are said and done so things keep going, they make it fun, and they make us laugh.

This ingredient to conversion is in our most basic doctrines.

- Alma calls on those who will be baptized to "bear one another's burdens, that they may be light" (Mosiah 18:8).
- The Lord through Moses commands Israel that "the stranger that dwelleth with you shall be as one born among you, and thou shalt love [her] as thyself" (Leviticus 19:34).
- Jesus says plainly in the Doctrine and Covenants: "Be one; and if ye are not one ye are not mine" (Doctrine and Covenants 38:27).

I DON'T FIT IN

When I was first called to serve in Relief Society, I was surprised at how many women sat down and told me: I'm not a "Relief Society" type. I'm not like everyone else. I'm not politically conservative, or I don't stay home. I'm not put together. My kids are in trouble. I'm twice divorced. I have sins I can't put to rest. I have doctrinal issues. Relief Society increases my anxiety.

I realized after a lot of this that none of us fits in.

Relief Society is exactly the place for all of us who don't fit in. It is organized under priesthood keys for women to have a place to grow, progress, build their faith, talk about the reality of family life, and mourn with each other for all the stupid, crazy things that happen to us when we are mortals. We cannot give in to those voices who say it's just like a sewing circle or a book club for people who have the same interests and backgrounds. No, Relief Society has a work to do on the earth. When you belong to Relief Society, you are part of that work. The Lord has a stewardship for his daughters in the work of salvation and only we can do it. It can only be done by women who are truly converted unto the Lord.

Sister Addie Fuhriman, who was on the Relief Society general board, said in 1980: "The Lord saw our similarities as well as our differences, and he valued both. And from that wisdom, he provided within the Church the Relief Society where gospel principles that can touch the heart and life of each woman—you, me, young, old, married or single . . .—could be taught."[11]

To Addie's list I would add: people with disabilities, recovering addicts, new in the church, old pioneer stock, American, Syrian, Chilean, Samoan, working, home with kids, wishing to have a job, poor, rich, in debt, happy, depressed, bipolar, autistic, serving others, being served, liberal, conservative, don't care, immigrant, gay, converted, and unconverted. The question is: Can we open up the circle of sisterhood to many more kinds of backgrounds and see those backgrounds as valuable instead of as handicaps?

I have a friend who is like this. She isn't shy. She makes friends easily. She can make anybody laugh. In any setting, she actively looks for the people who aren't part of the group and heads straight over to them. She's loyal. She's interested in all kinds of people and topics. It's extremely hard for her to give up on anyone. I tell her she has sticky hands. It's as if she has put glue on her hands and holds fast to the people she cares about. She's a good Samaritan. A seeker of black sheep. She bonds with people. She's an example to me of the tolerance and good will that glues the world together when people try.

In summary, the third ingredient of conversion is to: **Practice unity and love.** Strengthening our brethren and sisters shows how converted we ourselves are. These acts are often unseen or unrecognized but they last a very long time. Women who can do this are glue. It's the bonding together of the people around us and giving them relief for their problems that gives this block of conversion its power. It reaches us at the very core.

If the basic ingredients to our conversion are all the same, just like at the Asian cafe, the combinations of those ingredients are as endless as our personalities and spirits. Don't judge if I'm a rice bowl and you're a taco. We both contain the starch, protein, and flavor of the gospel. We are made from the same basic ingredients. Isn't it great she chose to put Korean BBQ sauce on her protein, and isn't it interesting you paired octopus with your starch?

Eyes to see, discipline to create, glue to bind. True conversion from these three basic ingredients isn't boring; it's endlessly interesting because it combines the building blocks of eternal life which are unchanging, "the same yesterday, today, and forever" (Mormon 9:9), with the infinite variety of each woman's completely unique personality. No one's conversion will be exactly like yours. And yet every one of them can be true.

If you look closely, you will notice that eyes to see, discipline to create, and glue to bind are expressed in Relief Society's purpose. Slightly different words but the same idea: Faith, Family, Relief.

Relief Society is designed as sort of a working kitchen to mix the ingredients of conversion. It is intended to take the work of salvation given particularly to women and create a structure for their expression and support. If we let it, it will make of us women who see beyond the barriers. It will help us repent and practice the discipline of creators. It will teach us to create something that didn't exist before. It honors the women who stand near the veil

to help us on our way, both going and coming. It acknowledges the invisible women who unify and make one, who serve the soup and cake, and who have sticky hands to hold people close to them. Relief Society is *faith*, it's *family*, and it's *relief.*

Relief Society is for all of us who don't fit in. It's the ultimate fit.

I would add just one note for when we sometimes get agitated and worry about the things women do or don't do. The second Relief Society General President, Eliza R. Snow, said this to the sisters: "We want to be ladies in very deed, not according to the term of the word as the world judges, but fit companions of the Gods and Holy Ones. In an organized capacity we can assist each other in not only doing good but in refining ourselves . . . Women should be women and not babies that need petting and correction all the time. I know we like to be appreciated but if we do not get all the appreciation which we think is our due, what matters? We know the Lord has laid high responsibility upon us, and there is not a wish or desire that the Lord has implanted in our hearts in righteousness but will be realized, and the greatest good we can do to ourselves and each other is to refine and cultivate ourselves in everything that is good and ennobling to qualify us for those responsibilities."[12]

In building our own conversions, we can personally seek the Savior, as Mary Magdalene did when she went to the tomb. We may not have the opportunity to see Him, but we can still witness of Christ. We can repent and obey the word of the Lord, like Mother Eve. We can discipline body and mind and use our godly powers for good and righteous examples, like the daughters of Onitah. Through the Holy Ghost we can learn the lessons our tragedies teach us, like Reyna Aburto. We can reach out with

glue on our hands and bring others into the circle or hold them as they pass back through the veil.

In conclusion, let me read the words of pure joy after Christ visited the people in the Americas and they were all converted and notice how much of true conversion results from taming contention. This comes from 4 Nephi 1:

"And it came to pass in the thirty and sixth year, the people were all converted unto the Lord, upon all the face of the land, both Nephites and Lamanites, and there were no contentions and disputations among them, and every man did deal justly one with another.

"And they had all things common among them; therefore there were not rich and poor, bond and free, but they were all made free, and partakers of the heavenly gift. . . .

"And there were no envyings, nor strifes, nor tumults, nor whoredoms, nor lyings, nor murders . . . and surely there could not be a happier people among all the people who had been created by the hand of God. . . . Neither were there Lamanites, nor any manner of -ites; but they were in one, the children of Christ, and heirs to the kingdom of God.

"And how blessed were they! For the Lord did bless them in all their doings; yea, even they were blessed and prospered" (4 Nephi 1:2–3, 16–18).

I testify that—exactly like the families in the Book of Mormon—if we build our conversion to the Lord, a little bit every day, by acting on our faith to see, by disciplining ourselves to repent and create according to the law, and by strengthening others in bonds of unity, the Lord will bless us in all our doings and we will find the happiness we seek.

THE HOPEFUL KEEP MOVING

Karen J. Ashton

Understanding my responsibility in speaking to this conference, I feel like Chorus, the character who begins each scene of Shakespeare's *Henry V*. Chorus must somehow engage the minds of the audience and help open a vision before them. He begins the first scene by saying:

> *O for a Muse of fire, that would ascend*
> *The brightest heaven of invention:*
> *A kingdom for a stage, princes to act,*
> *And monarchs to behold the swelling scene!*
> *. . . But pardon, gentles all,*
> *The flat unraisèd spirits that have dared*
> *On this unworthy scaffold to bring forth*
> *So great an object. . . .*
> *And let us, ciphers to this great account,*
> *On your imaginary forces work.*
> *. . . Think, when we talk of horses, that you see them, . . .*
> *For 'tis your thoughts that now must deck our kings,*
> *Carry them here and there, jumping o'er times,*

Turning th'accomplishment of many years
Into an hourglass . . .[1]

Like Chorus, I ask you to strip away the very walls and see the vast heavens above and around you. Envision the mighty galaxies rolling, churning on their onward paths as we hear the word of God to his sons, Moses and Abraham:

"And God spake unto Moses, saying: Behold, I am the Lord God Almighty, and Endless is my name; for I am without beginning of days or end of years; and is not this endless? . . . there is no God beside me, and all things are present with me, for I know them all. . . . And it came to pass that Moses looked, and beheld the world upon which he was created; and Moses beheld the world and the ends thereof, and all the children of men which are, and which were created; of the same he greatly marveled and wondered" (Moses 1:3, 6, 8).

And to God's faithful servant Abraham, God said, "For I am the Lord thy God; I dwell in heaven; the earth is my footstool; I stretch my hand over the sea, and it obeys my voice; I cause the wind and the fire to be my chariot; I say to the mountains— Depart hence—and behold, they are taken away by a whirlwind, in an instant, suddenly" (Abraham 2:7).

"And he said unto [Abraham]: My son, my son (and his hand was stretched out), behold I will show you all these. And he put his hand upon mine eyes, and I saw those things which his hands had made, which were many; and they multiplied before mine eyes, and I could not see the end thereof" (Abraham 3:12).

The Great Jehovah explained to Moses the reason for it all. "For behold, this is my work and my glory—to bring to pass the immortality and eternal life of man" (Moses 1:39).

Now we have a change of scene. We must return to the earth,

to a very small Sunday school room in Canada, where my husband and I sat with our missionaries and their investigators. Every Sunday, Brother Wilmont would begin his lesson by saying, "God made a plan! A plan of happiness, a plan of redemption, a plan of salvation and mercy." And then he would begin to draw a diagram. He would draw, at the top of the chalkboard, a large bubble that represented our premortal life and the great council in heaven. Then an arrow came down from the bubble, indicating The Fall, to a second bubble representing our second estate or our mortal experience. To the side of the second bubble, there were more lines, arrows, and bubbles representing the spirit world, resurrection, and judgment. The lines and arrows continued, pointing to a sun, a moon, and a star. Above the diagram stood a beautiful little figure representing the Savior who was overlooking the whole process. It was primitive, but very effective. Every week was the same: God made a plan! It was the foundation of every lesson and, by the end of the course, our investigators knew that God had made a plan.

But it was the second bubble in the diagram (our mortal experiences) that was everyone's greatest concern. That bubble could have consumed the entire board. In that bubble, there are so many ups and downs, bumps in the road, trials, tasks, and opportunities to be refined. When we left the Sunday school class, visions of glory and immortality vanished from our view because we were left looking at the reality of our lives. Many of us could have felt like Job when he said, "For the thing which I greatly feared is come upon me, and that which I was afraid of is come unto me" (Job 3:25).

This life is a test. It is a training. And it is a trial.

President Henry B. Eyring said, "The Lord doesn't put us through this test just to give us a grade; He does it because the process will change us."[2]

We must remember always that God knows what is happening to us and that he knew the end from the beginning. He loves us and will help us in every way.

Elder M. Russell Ballard said, "The Lord is in control. He knows the end from the beginning. He has given us adequate instruction that, if followed, will see us safely through any crisis. His purposes will be fulfilled, and someday we will all understand the eternal reasons for *all* these events."[3]

Come with me now to a lonely country road that stretches for miles straight through farm country. Picture an old blue, battered pickup truck with a fifteen-year-old girl behind the wheel and her father next to her on the front seat. I was the young girl. My father decided to teach me to drive at the age of fifteen so that I would be thoroughly prepared for my driver's education classes when I was sixteen. He explained the gas pedal to me along with the brake and the clutch. I was extremely confused. How was I supposed to use two feet on three pedals? He had me go up and down that lonely road over and over again, stopping, starting, gearing down, gearing up—and I started feeling pretty good about my driving abilities.

But then my dad took me to the big city—Salt Lake City—and I was a beginner all over again! There seemed to be a stop sign on every corner. I had to deal with other drivers—they were turning in front of me. They were slowing down my progress. Those other drivers, obviously, did not know how hard it was to drive that old truck! They would turn in front of me and slow down just as I was starting to speed up. I was not on the road alone. And the hills! Oh, the hills! Who would put a stop sign at the top of a hill? I knew that I would roll backwards several feet before I could give the engine enough gas to move forward.

This driving experience has become a metaphor for me in life. We are not in charge of what happens to us out on the roads of life. We are not in charge of the speed—only the direction. And because of conditions and what other people around us are doing, we will have to stop and start over and over again. We will have to slow down to accommodate change, to meet challenges, and to reevaluate our progress.

For me, first gear, or that place from which I begin, is always faith in the Lord Jesus Christ and in His Atonement; second gear is hope, the certainty that God will do what he has promised; and third gear is charity, the love of God and all mankind. Throughout my life, I had to return to first gear, or faith in the Lord Jesus Christ, over and over again.

Elder Ballard said, "Faith in the Lord Jesus Christ—real faith, whole-souled and unshakable—is a solid and unshakable power to be reckoned with in the universe. It can be the causative force through which miracles are wrought. Or it can be a source of inner strength through which we find peace, comfort, and courage to cope. As we put our faith and trust to work, hope is born."[4]

Even though we have faith and hope, sometimes things get so difficult that we are tempted to just pull to the side of the road and park. We lose faith. It may be that the difficulties or the rain that is falling so hard makes it impossible to see, and we can stumble into the most unwelcome place! Dr. Seuss, that wonderful philosopher of the twentieth century, spoke of this place in his book *Oh, the Places You'll Go!* He called it the waiting place, where you're forever waiting for something to happen instead of doing something to make things happen in your life.[5]

We *must* keep moving, even if we have to gear down again and again! But remember, first gear is always faith in the Lord

Jesus Christ. Waiting upon the Lord is not the absence of action or movement; it is acting upon what instruction and inspiration you've already received as you move forward in faith.

President Dieter F. Uchtdorf said, "Hope is not knowledge, but rather the abiding trust that the Lord will fulfill His promise to us. It is confidence that if we live according to God's law and the words of His prophets now, we will receive desired blessings in the future. It is believing and expecting that our prayers will be answered. It is manifest in confidence, optimism, enthusiasm, and patient perseverance. In the language of the gospel, this hope is sure, unwavering, and active."[6]

It is our faith and hope in the Lord Jesus Christ that enables us to move forward. He knows you, He loves you, and He planned for you to come here at this time in the world's history. He knows where you are and He knows what is happening in your life *right now!* With confidence, you can move forward.

President Uchtdorf also said, "Brothers and sisters, we are the Lord's 'little flock.' . . . As His covenant people, we need not be paralyzed by fear because bad things might happen. Instead, we can move forward with faith, courage, determination, and trust in God as we approach the challenges and opportunities ahead. We do not walk the path of discipleship alone. 'The Lord thy God . . . doth go with thee; he will not fail thee, nor forsake thee.' . . . God has promised, 'All things shall work together for your good, if [you] walk uprightly.' Therefore, let us set aside our fears and live instead with joy, humility, hope, and a bold confidence that the Lord is with us."[7]

I can testify that the Lord knows where you are and that He will come to your rescue and bless you when you are in need!

Come with me now to the teeming streets of Istanbul,

Turkey. It was the opportunity of a lifetime to travel with a group of BYU alumni and Daniel C. Peterson, a professor of Islamic studies and Arabic. We were going to see several of the ancient cities where the Apostle Paul ministered. Traveling always makes me slightly anxious, but I knew this was an opportunity in another way as well. I was serving at the time as a member of the Young Women general board and I had a chance to visit with the young women whose families were living in Istanbul. I made arrangements to meet with the small branch there and then Skype with the young women who lived outside the city.

After an afternoon of sightseeing in Istanbul, Sister Debbie Peterson (Dr. Peterson's wife) and I climbed into a taxi. We felt we had plenty of time to make it to my appointment. I was so grateful for Debbie's company. An hour later we were still crawling through traffic. The congestion was intense and the driver kept muttering to himself about something malfunctioning with the car. All of a sudden, he drove off the highway and down an exit. He yelled at us to get out of the taxi! Now keep in mind, he did not drop us off on the sidewalk; he dropped us off in the middle of the road. We had to make our way through traffic to the pedestrian area across the road, fending off cars with our hands as we walked.

There we were in the middle of Istanbul, two women from the United States unable to speak the language. We called the branch president. He asked us where we were. We had no idea. We described what we could see but finally he said, "Sisters, I'm so sorry. You will have to find someone who can tell you where the Metro is." He gave us the name of the stop where we should get off the Metro and hung up. Finding someone who could interpret our hand gestures would have been humorous if it had not been for the fact that we were now over an hour late for my appointment.

By the time we found the Metro, the sun was setting and it was getting dark in Istanbul. We secured our tickets and stepped into the overcrowded train. As the train sped along, I prayed that somehow we might find our way. Finally the doors opened and we spilled out. We moved with the crowd through the security gate, which locked behind us. Then, to our horror, we realized we were yet again in the wrong place! We searched our pockets for enough money to go back through the gate. You guessed it—no money. Now we were two women from the United States who could not speak Arabic, in the dark, with no money.

Just as we realized the full impact of our situation, a young man in a suit with a shaved head and sporting an incredibly shiny countenance walked down the empty exit ramp. He came directly to us and said to me, "How may I help you?"

We explained our situation. The young man turned us around and in Arabic explained to the guard what had happened. The guard opened the security gate and let us through. When we turned around to say thank you, the young man was gone.

Within minutes we found the correct exit and were met at the top of the ramp by a very patient Young Men's president who had been waiting there for hours.

When we know that God has a plan for us, that He will not leave us alone, that He knows where we are and that He will help us, we will continue to move forward.

With faith and hope, we will continue to repent, humbly acknowledging our weaknesses. The greatest battles we will ever fight are internal and, for the most part, unseen by anyone else; battles with selfishness, envy, jealousy, and pride.

Elder Jeffrey R. Holland said, "Please remember . . . that the Lord blesses those who *want* to improve, who accept the need for commandments and *try* to keep them, who cherish Christlike virtues and *strive* to the best of their ability to acquire them. If you stumble in that pursuit, so does everyone; the Savior is there to help you keep going. If you fall, summon His strength. Call out like Alma, 'O Jesus, . . . have mercy on me.' He will help you get back up. He will help you repent, repair, fix whatever you have to fix, and keep going. Soon enough you will have the success you seek."[8]

When we have faith and hope, we remain anxiously engaged in good causes, going about doing good as the Savior did. Our lives are filled with charity.

We are placed in what I have heard Sister Sheri Dew call 'personal orbits' that help us to bless each other. Several years ago, Elder Neal A. Maxwell spoke of this when he said, "Recall the new star that announced the birth at Bethlehem? It was in its precise orbit long before it so shone. We are likewise placed in human orbits to illuminate."[9]

There is someone out there today who will need your help, and into your life today someone will come who has the help you need, much like the angel who came to my rescue in Istanbul, Turkey.

When we have faith, hope, and charity, we will continue the work of the kingdom. We may have to slow down at times or even begin again, but we will go forward with a "steadfastness in Christ, having a perfect brightness of hope, and a love of God and of all men" (2 Nephi 31:20).

Elder Maxwell has also said, "Real hope keeps us 'anxiously engaged' in good causes even when these appear to be losing causes on the mortal scoreboard. . . . Real hope inspires quiet Christian service."[10]

Those of us who are filled with hope continue to fortify our families. We will continue to bring children into this life. We will not close up the womb in response to this evil that surrounds us.

Elder Maxwell said, "The truly hopeful . . . continue to work amid surrounding decay at having strong and happy families."[11]

We can hear God's voice in the scriptures urging us onward. His voice comforts us and sustains us. I have been mining in the scriptures for that very voice—the voice of love, affirmation, hope, and certainty. Here is just a small sample. Let these words flow over you:

- "Hearken unto me, ye that know righteousness, the people in whose heart I have written my law, fear ye not the reproach of men, neither be ye afraid of their revilings. . . . I am he; yea, I am he that comforteth you. Behold, who art thou, that thou shouldst be afraid of man, who shall die, and of the son of man, who shall be made like unto grass?" (2 Nephi 8:7, 12).
- "Be of good cheer . . . be not afraid" (Matthew 14:27).
- "Be not afraid of their faces: for I am with thee to deliver thee, saith the Lord" (Jeremiah 1:8).
- "For I, the Lord, have put forth my hand to exert the powers of heaven; ye cannot see it now, yet a little while and ye shall see it, and know that I am, and that I will come and reign with my people" (Doctrine and Covenants 84:119).
- "I have overcome the world" (John 16:33).
- "As you desire of me so it shall be done unto you" (Doctrine and Covenants 11:8).
- "Neither take ye thought beforehand what ye shall say; but treasure up in your minds continually the words of

life, and it shall be given you in the very hour that portion that shall be meted unto every man" (Doctrine and Covenants 84:85).

- "Whatsoever you desire of me [in] righteousness, *in faith believing in me* that you shall receive" (Doctrine and Covenants 11:14).
- "Therefore, sanctify yourselves that your minds become single to God, and the days will come that you shall see him; for he will unveil his face unto you" (Doctrine and Covenants 88:68).
- "And whoso receiveth you, there I will be also, for I will go before your face. I will be on your right hand and on your left, and my Spirit shall be in your hearts, and mine angels round about you, to bear you up" (Doctrine and Covenants 84:88).
- "Draw near unto me and I will draw near unto you; seek me diligently and ye shall find me; ask, and ye shall receive; knock, and it shall be opened unto you. Whatsoever ye ask the Father in my name it shall be given unto you, that is expedient for you" (Doctrine and Covenants 88:63–64).
- "All things work together for good to them that love God" (Romans 8:28).
- "Therefore, fear not, little flock; do good; let earth and hell combine against you, for if ye are built upon my rock, they cannot prevail" (Doctrine and Covenants 6:34).

As we complete our time together, we have one last change of scene. Please see with me again the heavens and listen to what God has in mind for those who continue in faith, hope, and charity:

"Hear, O ye heavens and give ear, O earth, and rejoice ye inhabitants thereof, for the Lord is God, and beside him there is no Savior.

"Great is his wisdom, marvelous are his ways, and the extent of his doing none can find out.

"His purposes fail not, neither are there any who can stay his hand. . . .

"For thus saith the Lord—I, the Lord, am merciful and gracious unto those who fear me, and delight to honor those who serve me in righteousness and in truth unto the end.

"Great shall be their reward and eternal shall be their glory.

"And to them will I reveal all mysteries, yea, all the hidden mysteries of my kingdom from days of old, and for ages to come, will I make known unto them the good pleasure of my will concerning all things pertaining to my kingdom.

"Yea, even the wonders of eternity shall they know, and things to come will I show them, even the things of many generations.

"And their wisdom shall be great, and their understanding reach to heaven; and before them the wisdom of the wise shall perish, and the understanding of the prudent shall come to naught.

"For by my Spirit will I enlighten them, and by my power will I make known unto them the secrets of my will—yea, even those things which eye has not seen, nor ear heard, nor yet entered into the heart of man" (Doctrine and Covenants 76:1–3, 5–10).

It is my testimony that I know that God, our Eternal Father, has a plan. I know that my Redeemer lives. I know that I shall see him again. I know that the young Joseph Smith, as a fourteen-year-old boy, saw God the Father and His Son. I know the gospel of Jesus Christ has been restored on the earth. Because of this, I can move forward with great faith, hope, and charity.

HOW VAST IS OUR PURPOSE

Jean B. Bingham

As I began to get to know my counselors, these two stellar women, Sister Sharon Eubank and Sister Reyna I. Aburto, who are so capable and full of faith, I'll be honest: I felt a bit intimidated. As those who know me well are aware, my story is quite ordinary. Growing up, although I enjoyed learning, I was not the top student in any class. I cannot boast of any expert skills: I play the piano, but only enough to stumble through a hymn. I love to visit art museums to see the paintings and sculptures by great masters, yet my artistic talents were limited to doodling designs in my notebooks. I learned to sew a wearable skirt, but tailoring a suit was definitely beyond my ability. Although I was blessed with good health and loved to run through the park or swim in the lake, I didn't participate in school sports at any level. I was never asked to the prom, I wasn't the president of anything, I was never one of the popular group, and one strikingly attractive friend said to me after scrutinizing my features, "Well, you'll never be beautiful, but you could be cute." In other words, I was just average.

Some of you may relate to these kinds of experiences, feeling that you are also "just average." Have you ever felt ordinary, maybe even less than average? If you're human—and particularly, a female human—you have probably experienced those times of self-doubt and discouragement that you are not all that you want to be.

And yet, even in my "ordinariness," Heavenly Father saw value, and has helped me begin to develop the gifts and graces He knows will help me become all that He has designed me to be. Know that your Heavenly Father will provide all that *you* need to become "extra"-ordinary as a daughter of God. The wonder of His heavenly economy is that every single one of us can be spectacular because of our unique bundle of talents and abilities. Unlike the world, in His kingdom there is no winner's platform that only has room for one or two. *Each* of His daughters has been taught and prepared and gifted premortally with marvelous potential to become a queen in the celestial kingdom.

What do you want to accomplish in your life? What are your goals and aspirations? If your long-term goal is to enter the celestial kingdom to live with our Heavenly Parents and with loved family members forever, that singular focus will take you farther than you now think is possible. We are promised, "Eye hath not seen, nor ear heard, neither have entered into the heart of man [or woman], the things which God hath prepared for them that love him" (1 Corinthians 2:9).

You have incredible potential for good because you are a covenant daughter of Heavenly Parents. The evidence of your inherent potential for greatness is the simple fact that you were born on the earth because you made the choice in the premortal world to accept Heavenly Father's plan of salvation and to follow the example of His Son, Jesus Christ. And because Jesus Christ was willing to take upon Himself the sins and infirmities (Alma 7:11–13)—or inadequacies—of each of us, and fulfilled that sacred trust through His Infinite Atonement, we can have every confidence that we can become all we were divinely designed to be. As we make and keep sacred covenants, we demonstrate our desire to fulfill that divine potential.

Answer this question: Do you think our Heavenly Parents want us to succeed? Yes! They want us to succeed gloriously! And do you think They will help us? Absolutely! We know that God's "work and glory is to bring to pass the immortality"—which has already been accomplished through the Savior's Atonement and resurrection—"and eternal life of man" (Mosiah 1:39). His goal is for every single one of us to return to our eternal home, having increased the talents and gifts with which He blesses us through our obedience and perseverance during this mortal life. We know we cannot do this on our own, but through Heavenly Father's love and the Savior's grace, we can accomplish all that is required for exaltation.

That thought sustained me when I was called to be the Relief Society General President. Knowing that I do not have all the wisdom and ability to fulfill what will be required, I nevertheless take comfort and strength from the knowledge that God "has all wisdom, and all power, both in heaven and in earth" (Mosiah 4:9), and if we just try, just do our best, imperfect as that will be, the Lord will be on our right hand and on our left, and angels will bear us up (see Doctrine and Covenants 84:88). All He requires is "the heart and a willing mind" (Doctrine and Covenants 64:34), and as we are obedient to His commandments, we will be strengthened to accomplish all that is required in this life as well as entrance into His kingdom in the life hereafter. That choice to become a disciple of Christ gives us the opportunity to wield a more-than-might-be-expected influence on those around us.

Every one of us has this same promise and potential. It matters not where we live, the makeup of our family, the size of our bank account, whether we are a world-class expert in some field, or how long we have been a member of the Church—we can each be a powerful influence for good. Living with integrity at home and in the community, using a gentle voice and kind words with a challenging child or difficult co-worker, demonstrating your standards by your modest way of dressing, reaching out of your comfort zone to become acquainted with those who live around you—there are many simple actions we can do that will influence others to also rise to a higher plane.

I recently read this statement by a woman leader of the Church. Who do you think said this? "Never have women had greater influence than in today's world. Never have the doors of opportunity opened wider for them. This is an inviting, exciting, challenging, and demanding period of time for women. It is a time rich in rewards if we keep our balance, learn the true values of life, and wisely determine priorities."[1] That was Belle S. Spafford, in 1974, who was the general Relief Society president for over thirty years! Interestingly, her statement is just as true today.

So, what will we do with this time of great opportunity and challenge? "How vast *is* our purpose, how broad is our mission"?[2]

Those of you who are familiar with the history of the settlement of frontier areas around the world know that many towns began as haphazard gatherings of rough men who came to do business and find their fortunes. It wasn't until women arrived in increasing numbers and insisted on establishing churches and schools and an orderly environment that real progress was made on what could be called civilized living. Elder D. Todd

Christofferson explained this process and the reasons why: "From age immemorial, societies have relied on the moral force of women. While certainly not the only positive influence at work in society, the moral foundation provided by women has proved uniquely beneficial to the common good. Perhaps, because it is pervasive, this contribution of women is often underappreciated. . . . Women bring with them into the world a certain virtue, a divine gift that makes them adept at instilling such qualities as faith, courage, empathy, and refinement in relationships and in cultures."[3]

Women are given gifts that allow them to see the details as well as the big picture, often at the same time. Discover those gifts and use them, dear sisters!

I remember President James E. Faust telling us in his rich yet humble voice, "You sisters do not know the full extent of your influence. You sisters enrich all of humanity. . . . Each woman brings her own separate, unique strengths to the family and the Church. Being a daughter of God means that if you seek it, you can find your true identity. You will know who you are. This will make you free—not free from restraints, but free from doubts, anxieties, or peer pressure. You will not need to worry, 'Do I look all right?' 'Do I sound OK?' 'What do people think of me?' A conviction that you are a daughter of God gives you a feeling of comfort in your self-worth. It means that you can find strength in the balm of Christ. It will help you meet heartaches and challenges with faith and serenity."[4]

So, who *are* we as Relief Society sisters? Although each woman is unique, there are feelings and divine gifts and experiences that we have in common which bind us together. We are daughters of our Heavenly Parents, who love us and want us to become like Them. We are full partners with the priesthood in the work of salvation—the saving of the souls of men and women—which is the focus of all our efforts. As sisters and brothers, we were given and accepted responsibilities in the premortal world for building the Kingdom of God on the earth. Speaking of the "noble and great ones" (that's you!), "Even before they were born, they, with many others, received their first lessons in the world of spirits and were prepared to come forth in the due time of the Lord to labor in his vineyard for the salvation of the souls of men" (Doctrine and Covenants 138:55–56).

As Emma Smith, the first Relief Society president, phrased it in 1842, "We are going to do something extraordinary[!]"[5] You may not realize it yet, but Relief Society can help you accomplish extraordinary things.

What does Relief Society mean to *you*? As adult female members of The Church of Jesus Christ of Latter-day Saints, you and I belong to one of the oldest and largest women's organizations in the world. With more than 7.1 million sisters around the globe, we have a bond that can be eternal.

Relief Society is more than a class on Sunday. "It is a divinely established sisterhood. [It] is a place of learning. . . . It is an organization whose basic charter is caring for others. [Our] motto is "Charity Never Faileth."[6] "[Relief Society] provides a home away from [our] heavenly home, where [we] can fellowship with others who share [our] beliefs and values."[7] It is a safe place for sisters to bring their questions and for those who are searching for identity and purpose. It is a place that will help us blossom individually and improve collectively.

What does Relief Society mean to me? Relief Society has changed over the years—and has changed *me* over the years! To paraphrase, "It's not just your grandma's Relief Society." When I left home to go to college, I automatically became a member of Relief Society. I gathered with other young women my age to learn the gospel and to serve others in an organized way. My first callings were as a Relief Society teacher and a visiting teacher. It was easy to knock on the door of an apartment in my complex and to chat with the girls who were of my similar age and circumstance.

Later, as a brand-new mother, I was called to teach Relief Society mother education classes. My circle was expanded as the women in my new ward accepted me with open hearts and provided great examples as role models of faithful sisters who valued motherhood and delighted in their role, as well as those who were pursuing education or were employed and established in a career. It was more challenging to visit teach because of the distances involved, but I was blessed to be visited by women who genuinely cared about me and showed me how to extend that love to other sisters who were in different stages of life than mine.

As a more mature (read "aging") woman, my circle has been expanded yet again to include many younger than myself. Now I am the "experienced" one who can share my hard-earned insights as well as be invigorated by younger sisters who are enthusiastic about what lies ahead. Over the years, I have learned to be persistent in contacting less-active sisters whom I have been given to visit, and because of our common experiences as women, have found wonderful friends that have enriched my life. As I work to express the Savior's love through serving them in ways that are meaningful to them, their hearts soften and they often become receptive to the Spirit.

There have also been bumps and challenges along the way.

Not every interaction at Relief Society has been perfect. There have been women who were insensitive to my feelings, who didn't respond to me in a Christlike way, and on the other hand, I'm sure I have been the cause of unintended hurt to some of my sisters in the gospel. One experience was so painful that I wanted to move to another city to avoid any more trauma and drama! Yet each time, in remembering the example of our Savior, Jesus Christ, the "eyes of [my] understanding were opened" (Doctrine and Covenants 110:1), and through His grace, I came to genuinely love and enjoy those sisters who had heretofore been difficult for me to appreciate. If you have had a less-than-comfortable experience at Relief Society, remember that we are all learning, so persist in loving your sisters.

And what do we *do* as Relief Society sisters? If you are familiar with the updated Relief Society purpose statement, you know that "Relief Society helps prepare women for the blessings of eternal life as they increase faith in Heavenly Father and Jesus Christ and His Atonement; strengthen individuals, families, and homes through ordinances and covenants; and work in unity to help those in need."[8]

So, number one, we work to fulfill our divine potential. To do that, we "all work together" . . . to love, "to cheer and to bless in [the Savior's] name."[9] We participate in the work of salvation, which "includes member missionary work, convert retention, activation of less-active members, temple and family history work, and teaching the gospel"[10]—all things which you are already doing. All baptized members of the Church, including children, participate in this work, which is accomplished with steady effort, a bit at a time, in the family and the workplace or school, the neighborhood and the community—anywhere and everywhere we have an influence.

And where and how do we do this work? As we put our arm around a shy sister at church, as we reach out to a young woman who is struggling, as we work to feed and clothe and teach a child on a daily basis, as we share what makes us happy about the restored gospel with our neighbor, as we mourn with someone who has lost a loved one, as we attend the temple at an inconvenient time, as we help a refugee navigate the bewildering array in a grocery store, as we expend effort in learning and developing our talents with the goal of being an instrument for the Lord, as we patiently tutor a new member who is learning to do family history, as we prepare to teach a Primary or seminary class—all of these actions and many more acts of simple but meaningful service are part of the work of salvation. *That* is our mission, and it truly is vast, but it *is doable* when we each do something—and keep at it!

For instance, a busy young mother in Arizona wondered what she could do to help a newly arrived refugee family in her community in some small way. She soon learned that she could help furnish a few articles for their empty apartment. When she and her children visited the family to bring the articles, she realized that the mother had no purse to carry her personal items. And a woman needs a purse! She knew that she and many of her friends had extra purses that could be useful to these women, so she sent out a request on social media. That simple beginning has blossomed into a warehouse full of items needed by just-arriving families and has also become the means of providing many community members with a welcome opportunity to give of themselves, as well as creating a sweet bond between these women of different faiths.

Sister Eliza R. Snow, the second general Relief Society president, testified, "If any of the daughters and mothers in Israel are feeling in the least [limited] in their present spheres, they will now find ample scope for every power and capability for doing good with which they are most liberally endowed."[11]

So, what "extraordinary thing" will you choose to do? Choose something according to your available time and resources. "Do not run faster or labor more than you have strength and means . . . but be diligent" (Doctrine and Covenants 10:4). Whether your "work of salvation" is largely in the home at this time in life or your influence extends to a global scale, or somewhere in between, the Lord is pleased with your efforts when you are focused on serving God's children and the eternal goal of returning to Him as a "new and improved" version of your spiritual self. As President Dieter F. Uchtdorf phrased it so succinctly, "Exaltation is our goal; discipleship is our journey."[12]

As we go forward in this journey of discipleship, may we each determine to reach out in small and simple ways that bless our families and others in *extra*-ordinary ways. May we each treasure our relationships in this divinely designed organization, and come to know and follow Jesus Christ whose teachings and perfect example will lead us back to our Heavenly Father.

LIVING IN GRACE

Emily Belle Freeman

Many years ago, Elder M. Russell Ballard attended our stake conference. Our family was in the satellite building, watching the broadcast on a large screen. Just before the meeting ended, it was announced that Elder Ballard would come and share a few thoughts at our building, and we were asked to sit quietly and wait while he traveled to us. Someone began playing the organ and we quietly prepared for an apostle to enter the chapel.

After a few minutes my young daughter Megan leaned over and asked, "What are we doing?"

It was a little confusing, I realized. We had sung the last song and someone had given the closing prayer, two clear signs for the meeting to end and for everyone to get up and leave, and yet we were all still sitting quietly in our seats. I leaned over and whispered, "We are waiting for Elder Ballard to come speak."

"We just saw him speak," she said, pointing up to the large screen.

"I know," I replied, "but now we get to hear him speak in real life."

"Why do we want to hear him speak in real life?" she asked,

her wide eyes innocent in their questioning, her small self all tired out from sitting for so long already.

"Because he is an apostle of the Lord," I patiently told her. "We want to hear him speak because he will tell us what Jesus would tell us if He was here."

"How does he know what Jesus would tell us?" She questioned.

"Because he talks to Jesus," I answered.

"Wait," Megan replied, wide-eyed and curious, "you mean Jesus is *real?*"

It was one of those moments when it is extremely clear you are not going to win Mother of the Year and you realize that, clearly, there is a lot more teaching to be done.

Maybe each of us have moments when we question our understanding and belief in the reality of the Savior. Perhaps the greatest quest of our lives is discovering how Jesus Christ can become real to us, how we can live more fully through His grace, and how we come to know Him. "How then shall they call on him in whom they have not believed? and how shall they believe in him of whom they have not heard?" (Romans 10:14). Paul teaches us that in order to know the Lord we must believe in Him, and the best way to come to believe is to hear about Him.

One of the best ways to "hear" about Jesus Christ is to turn to the New Testament. Within those pages we are able to learn from His interaction with ordinary people in everyday situations. In John 8 we read of a woman who is thrown at the feet of the Lord. As you read through these verses, try to picture this scene in your mind. Don't focus as much on the words, focus on the movement of both the woman and the Savior.

"And early in the morning he came again into the temple, and all the people came unto him; and *he sat down*, and taught them. And the scribes and Pharisees brought unto him a woman taken in adultery; and when they had *set her in the midst*, they say unto him, Master, this woman was taken in adultery, in the very act. Now Moses in the law commanded us, that such should be stoned: but what sayest thou? This they said, tempting him, that they might have to accuse him. *But Jesus stooped down*, and with his finger wrote on the ground, as though he heard them not. So when they continued asking him, *he lifted up himself*, and said unto them, He that is without sin among you, let him first cast a stone at her. *And again he stooped down*, and wrote on the ground. And they which heard it, being convicted by their own conscience, went out one by one, beginning at the eldest, even unto the last: and Jesus was left alone, and *the woman standing in the midst*. When Jesus *had lifted up himself*, and saw none but the woman, he said unto her, Woman, where are those thine accusers? hath no man condemned thee? She said, No man, Lord. And Jesus said unto her, Neither do I condemn thee: go, and sin no more" (John 8:2–11; emphasis added; paragraphing altered.)

One of the most profound lessons of this story isn't found in what Jesus said; it is discovered in what He did. We see how He stood up to talk to the accusers, but He bent down to speak with her. He met her on her level. Where she was. As she was. He did not condemn her but instead offered His grace. This is the character of Christ. If we look carefully we see it in other New Testament stories. When Peter was trying to walk on water, Jesus wasn't on the shore shouting out instructions or in the boat giving encouragement. He was *in* the water. With Peter. Where he was. It is the same with Nicodemus; Jesus met him where he was, in the dark of night. In secret. The lame man, the woman at the well, the leper, all testify of this truth. It didn't matter where they were—beside a pool of water, at a well in the heat of the day, or in a colony, Jesus met them where they were, as they were. It is His way. There is a powerful lesson there.

For the past few months our family has been studying grace. One Easter weekend we all gathered to have a discussion on grace and how it works in our lives. Our dear friends who live next door came over with their whole family to join the conversation. We extended a challenge for everyone to spend one week living in grace. One of the girls raised her hand and said, "I don't understand how this works. I feel like I have to 'do' something before I can receive grace."

I knew what she was referring to, the familiar scripture on grace found in 2 Nephi 25:23, "For we labor diligently to write, to persuade our children, and also our brethren, to believe in Christ, and to be reconciled to God; for we know that it is by grace that we are saved, *after all we can do*" (emphasis added).

Immediately I thought about the woman caught in adultery. What did she really *do*? What qualified *her* to receive grace? She was caught in sin and thrown at the feet of the Savior. She didn't do anything and still grace was given. The Lord met her where she was, as she was, and extended His grace to her.

My mind started to review other favorite New Testament stories. I thought about Saul on the road to Damascus, what did he do to qualify for grace? He was on his way to persecute the followers of Christ. Next I remembered the woman at the well. She hadn't really done anything significant, she simply came to the well to perform an ordinary daily responsibility. And what about the lame man at Bethesda who laid waiting by a pool that couldn't heal him for thirty-eight years?

Did any of these people actually *do* something before the Savior extended His grace?

The stories in the New Testament are clear, the Lord met them where they were—on a path intent to destroy, in a moment of ordinary duty and work, beside a pool hoping for healing—and offered a better way through grace. In that moment, I realized something important. Grace is less about what *we* do, and more about what *He* will do because of what He has already done. The gift of grace is offered to everyone, everywhere. That is the lesson we learn over and over again as we turn to scriptures about Him. The Lord will meet us where we are, as we are, but He doesn't intend to leave us there. His grace has the power to transform us into something better.

Think of the invitations he extended to those who had been touched by His grace. To the woman caught in adultery, "Go, and sin no more" (John 8:11). To the lame man at the pool of Bethesda, "Rise, take up thy bed and walk" (John 5:8). To Saul on the road to Damascus, "Go into the city, and it shall be told thee what thou must do" (Acts 9:6). And to the woman sitting at the well, "Drink of the water I shall give" (John 4:1–42).

These are the kind of invitations that have the power to transform a life. They remind me what Elder Jeffrey R. Holland said in his April 2017 general conference talk, "'Come as you are,' a loving Father says to each of us, but He adds, 'Don't plan to stay as you are.'"[1] The work of the Lord is to transform us through His grace. He doesn't wait for us to earn that grace. He offers it to us in our most imperfect moments—when we are at our weakest. "My grace is sufficient for thee: for my strength is made perfect in weakness" (2 Corinthians 12:9). Consider that definition of grace: His strength made complete in our weakness. It is a powerful truth, and if it is true in the New Testament, then it is true for each of us.

Take a few minutes to think about this: *Where has He met you? What did you learn about Him there?* Maybe you will write those memories down. Perhaps you will record the lessons learned. Through that process, through the reflection of those personal experiences, we will each come to understand His grace and how it works in our life.

I love the story of Nathanael found in John 1. The apostles went to find Nathanael, to tell him they had found the Messiah, who the prophets testified would come. When Nathanael asked who He was, the apostles explained that it was Jesus of Nazareth, the son of Joseph. Immediately Nathanael replied, "Can there any good thing come out of Nazareth?" (John 1:46). So they went to find Jesus, and when Jesus saw Nathanael coming he said, "Behold an Israelite indeed, in whom is no guile!" (John 1:47). Nathanael replied, "Whence knowest thou me?" Jesus immediately answered with an interesting reply, "When thou wast under the fig tree, I saw thee" (John 1:48).

It is Nathanael's next response that is the most intriguing. Before reading it, consider this: How many fig trees are in Jerusalem? And how many people do you think spend time sitting under those trees? It feels like it would be such a common occurrence to see someone sitting under a fig tree. And yet, instead of responding with something casual, "Oh, of course, yes, I think I remember seeing you pass by," Nathanael says this, "Rabbi, *thou art the Son of God*; thou art the King of Israel" (John 1:49; emphasis added). Why? What happened under the fig tree? It must have been something significant. Perhaps something only Nathanael and God knew about. A private and sacred experience.

A moment that solidified in Nathanael's heart exactly who Jesus was.

Have you had a fig-tree experience? Something only you and the Lord know about? A time when He met you where you were, as you were? A moment that let you know more about the character of Christ?

I love what happens just after Nathanael declares, "Thou art the son of God." Jesus answers and says, "Because I said unto thee, I saw thee under the fig tree, believest thou? thou shalt see greater things than these" (John 1:50). That is the beautiful thing about grace. When we receive His grace, in those private and personal experiences, we will be led to discover greater things. The more we turn again to Him, the more grace we will receive. "Line upon line, precept upon precept" (Doctrine and Covenants 98:12). It is through the continual process of turning to Him and receiving the gift of grace that we become transformed.

Let's consider again the familiar scripture on grace found in 2 Nephi 25:23, "For we labor diligently to write, to persuade our children, and also our brethren, to believe in Christ, and to be reconciled to God; for we know that it is by grace that we are saved, *after all we can do*" (emphasis added).

Many people have tried to define what is meant by "all we can do." My favorite definition of "all we can do" actually comes from the man who gave the sermon in 2 Nephi 25—from Nephi himself. Take a few minutes to read Nephi's entire sermon. As you read, focus on verses 16–30; here you will find that he repeats one invitation seven times:

- "They shall be persuaded *to believe in Christ,* the son of God, and the atonement, which is infinite for all mankind" (2 Nephi 25:16; emphasis added).

- "They shall *believe in Christ*" (2 Nephi 25:16; emphasis added).
- "We labor diligently to write, to persuade our children, and also our brethren, *to believe in Christ*" (2 Nephi 25:23; emphasis added).
- "We *believe in Christ*" (2 Nephi 25:24; emphasis added).
- "We talk of Christ, we rejoice in Christ, we preach of Christ, we prophesy of Christ, and we write according to our prophecies, that our children may to know what source they must look" (2 Nephi 25:26).
- "For the right way is to *believe in Christ*" (2 Nephi 25:28; emphasis added).
- "And the right way is to *believe in Christ*" (2 Nephi 25:29; emphasis added).

Nephi actually explains the complicated phrase on his own: All we can do is *believe in Christ.*

In his talk "The Gift of Grace," given in the April 2015 general conference, President Dieter F. Uchtdorf explained, "The prophet Nephi made an important contribution to our understanding of God's grace when he declared, 'We labor diligently . . . to persuade our children, and also our brethren, to believe in Christ, and to be reconciled to God; for we know that it is *by grace that we are saved, after all we can do*' (2 Nephi 25:23; emphasis added). However, I wonder if sometimes we misinterpret the phrase 'after all we can do.' We must understand that 'after' does not equal 'because.' We are not saved 'because' of all that we can do. Have any of us done *all* that we can do? Does God wait until we've expended every effort before He will intervene in our lives with His saving grace? Many people feel discouraged because they constantly fall short. . . . I am certain Nephi knew that the Savior's grace *allows* and *enables* us to overcome sin (see 2 Nephi 4:19–35; Alma 34:31). This is why Nephi labored so diligently to persuade his children and brethren 'to believe in Christ, and to be reconciled to God' (2 Nephi 25:23). After all, *that is* what we can do!"[2]

Again, I find myself thinking back to our Easter Sunday conversation when my darling neighbor expressed her concern, "I feel like I have to do something." It is true, we have to do something—we have to believe. Often when I explain that to people they reply, "That can't be it. It's too simple. We have to do more than just believe." However, we must remember that *belief* isn't an idle word, a standing by. It isn't just a vocal expression and then a wait and see. It is a powerful action word that when used to its fullest potential can lead to the "greater things" Jesus told Nathanael about.

In order to understand the word belief, it helps to define what true belief looks like. I love the story of Jehoshaphat found in the Old Testament in 2 Chronicles 20. The Ammonites were coming against Jehoshaphat to battle—a great multitude, a giant army. King Jehoshaphat was scared, and set himself to seek the Lord, and proclaimed a fast throughout all Judah. All of his people gathered themselves together to ask help of the Lord. I love where they gathered. They stood in front of the temple, and Jehoshaphat began to pray, "O Lord God of our fathers . . . [we] have built thee a sanctuary therein for thy name, saying, If, when evil cometh upon us, as the sword, judgment, or pestilence, or famine, we stand before this house, and in thy presence, (for thy name is in this house,) and cry unto thee in our affliction, then thou wilt hear and help. . . . O our God . . . we have no might against this great company that cometh against us; neither know we what to do: but our eyes are upon thee. And all Judah stood before the Lord, with their little ones, their wives, and their children. Then

. . . came the Spirit of the Lord in the midst of the congregation; and he said . . . Be not afraid nor dismayed by reason of this great multitude; for the battle is not yours, but God's. . . . Ye shall not need to fight in this battle: set yourselves, stand ye still, and see the salvation of the Lord. . . . Fear not, nor be dismayed . . . for the Lord will be with you" (2 Chronicles 20:6–17).

Then Jehoshaphat stood and said, "Hear me O Judah, and ye inhabitants of Jerusalem: Believe in the Lord your God, so shall ye be established" (2 Chronicles 20:20).

What did the people of Jehoshaphat have to do for grace to come? *Believe.* But it wasn't a passive response; it was a belief that moved them to action. They fasted, went to the temple, prayed. Oh, there are so many lessons in this powerful story! There will be times when tribulation will come upon us. Just like Jehoshaphat, we will say, Lord, we know not what to do. We will petition with our little ones, our spouses, our children. And then, we must believe. The power of that belief will enable us to be established, to fear not, to be not afraid, to stand still, because of our unfailing certainty that the Lord will be with us. It will allow us to experience His grace in the form of an enabling power, a divine means of help or strength.[3] True belief can be powerful, and it will allow us to live in grace.

Grace can instill in us the power to change. That transformation is one of the most beautiful aspects of the gift of grace. The Greek word for grace is *charis. Strong's Concordance* defines the word *charis* as "the divine influence upon the heart and its reflection in the life."[4] When we receive and then reflect grace we become a better version of ourselves. We are transformed into a better mother, a better friend, a better spouse. But how does it really work?

Many years ago my husband, Greg, was driving down the street on his way to a job. He passed a home where a family we knew well was packing up all of their belongings and preparing to move. Their third son was standing on the curb with all of his belongings. None of those belongings were being placed into the moving truck. Immediately my husband knew what was happening. This boy was a troubled kid. He had spent time in jail. He was known by our local police department on a first-name basis. Things had been really rough in his home for years, and it was clear that he had been asked to find somewhere else to go. Perhaps you have heard me tell the story before—how Greg loaded all of his belongings into the back of his truck. How the Lord whispered to my heart to bring him home. How we set up boundaries, and rules, and how, slowly, things began to change. The changing wasn't easy. For every step forward there were two steps back, reworking the boundaries, relearning the rules. Overcoming addictions doesn't come easy, and often requires turning again and again back to the Lord. Along the way there were ups and downs, including leaving to serve a mission and then coming home early. It was a continual process, this turning again and again back to the Lord, picking himself back up every time he fell. But all along, there was grace. I will never forget one of the hardest days. He was about to return home from his LDS mission early. The day was filled with prayer—"What should we do with Garett?" That night my husband and I visited a museum showcasing paintings of Christ. I stood in front of one painting for most of the evening, pouring my heart out in prayer. Over and over I petitioned the Lord, "What should we do with Garett?" and over and over, the response came back, "Just love him." I remember answering, "I do love him, but what should we *do* with him?" Where should he live? Where will he work? What will he do for the rest of his life? I wanted a to-do list, but the answer from the Lord kept coming back clear, "Just love him." And so we did.

Over the years we watched the Lord at work. The journey that began with a police record, a jail stay, addictions, and a boy standing on a curb would end with a boy who learned from his mistakes, picked himself up, and attended junior college to play football. That led to a year playing football at a Division I college, and then an invitation to play in the NFL. He was one of twenty-two players invited to the first-round NFL draft in April of 2017. He was drafted in the first round, at number twenty, to play for the Denver Broncos. Perhaps you have seen *The Blind Side*—it is Garett's favorite movie. But Garett's story is a little bit different. It's not about a troubled boy or the woman who brought him home. It's about grace.

You see, it was the Lord who met Garett on the curb that day, but He didn't intend to leave him there. He helped guide him to the right people in the right places to get him to the place where God could perform His great work in him. The list of those God-sent people would fill up pages and pages: coaches, special education teachers, support specialists, neighbors, family members. I feel blessed that Greg and I happened to be two of the people on God's list. The blessing of being Garett's mom has changed me. It has transformed my own life.

The other day a man stopped me as I was walking through a parking lot. He asked about Garett—he had seen that we were going to the draft in Philadelphia and wanted to offer his congratulations. Then he said, "Can I ask you something?"

"Sure," I replied.

"We're doing something similar to you," he said. "Brought some kids into our home; we're trying to raise them right. I see you where you are now, and it's a great story. But I have to ask you something." He looked at me, serious now, the smile gone from his face. "I hope you don't mind if I ask you this," his eyes squinted in question, and then he continued, "Was it hard? *Please say it was hard.*"

I couldn't stop the tears from gathering in my eyes as my mind flashed back over those beginning years. "It's the hardest thing I've ever done," I told him. I didn't have to explain why. He knew. *He already knew.*

You know, I often look back to that night in the museum. The night I prayed to God, asking what to do with Garett. The night I wanted a to-do list, and how clear the answer was, "Just love him." Had the Lord told me, "Oh, don't you worry about him. He'll attend college and be on the honor roll. He will be a successful football player. He will marry a beautiful girl, they will be sealed in the temple, and he will be a fantastic father." I would have chuckled, and then asked again: "No, really. What should we do with Garett?" Heavenly Father knew my heart couldn't even comprehend the great things He had in store if Garett would turn to Him and rely on grace.

My most favorite moment of the NFL draft was the moment Garett stood on the stage with his son, Kingston, in one hand and his Broncos jersey in the other and simply said, "I'm here by the grace of God." And it is true. His life was transformed by grace. Not simply in the moment he stood on that stage, but every single moment that led up to it.

I am a firm believer in this scripture, "By the grace of God I am what I am: and his grace which was bestowed upon me was not in vain; but I laboured more abundantly than they all: yet not I, but the grace of God which was with me" (1 Corinthians 15:10).

The Lord will meet us where we are, as we are, but He doesn't intend to leave us there. Through grace He will transform us into the person we are meant to become. His grace can be with us in every moment of every day if we just believe.

Believe in Him.

Believe in who we can become through Him.

That is what it means to live in grace.

"WHY DO YOU STAY?"

Barbara Morgan Gardner

One of my favorite aspects of being a religion professor at Brigham Young University is the opportunity it gives me to talk primarily with young adult members of the Church regarding their testimonies, experiences, frustrations, hopes, dreams, struggles, losses, and successes. I have been overjoyed as I have seen students, friends, family, colleagues, and neighbors exercise their faith and make it through difficult trials stronger and more determined and grounded in the gospel of Jesus Christ. I have also been concerned, saddened, frustrated, and even at times felt defeated as I have watched students, friends, family, colleagues, and neighbors fall away.

Perhaps because, like the sons of Mosiah, I, like many of you, cannot stand the idea of even one soul being lost, I began my own personal study of scriptures and talks and conducted interviews to find out why people leave the Church and why people stay—and how we can help. In my research, it seems that many have written and discussed various reasons as to why people leave the Church, but found very little research discussing why people stay. In my interviews, therefore, I began looking for people who had difficult life experiences they were dealing with that had caused other people to leave the Church, but these members stayed. Typically, after interviewing these members about their experiences, mostly difficult and heart-wrenching, I would simply ask, "So why are you staying?" The answers varied, although there are some extremely important similarities. I'll share a few of my experiences as I interviewed these members.

EXPERIENCES

1. With two cups of water in my hand, I sat down at the BYU Creamery across from a student who took me up on an invitation to go with me to lunch. I invite my students every semester to come to lunch and I typically get about two takers. Little do they know it could really help their grade, but that's for them to figure out. "So how was your mission?" I asked this student nonchalantly. "I was raped," came her simple, seemingly emotionless response. "That's partially why I want to talk to you," she continued. My own emotions were scattered as I sat quietly intrigued as she expressed in dignified detail her experience of just a few months back.[1]

2. I quickly glanced down at a text message that came through as I was driving home. "Is this Sister Morgan?" was the simple query. "Yes" was my quick response. "I'm sorry to bother you, but I have a few questions and I'm wondering if you would have a second to talk?" After replying in the affirmative, and having pulled into my driveway, I returned the call. "I have heard and read and studied so much information regarding the prophet Joseph Smith lately. There are so many things I was never taught in seminary or as an undergraduate student at BYU or in Sunday school. Why has the Church been keeping this information from us?"

"Women's issues in the church are so frustrating," she explained intently after our Eternal Family class. "The temple is so confusing and feels so demeaning towards women. It seems that we are told one thing in one setting and shown something completely different in another. Why is there so much confusion regarding women?"

3. I looked around to find his companion as I watched this young missionary stumble across the street and print his boarding pass at Delta terminal at the Salt Lake Airport. "Can I help you?" was my simple inquiry. With tears in his eyes, he cried, "They dropped me off at the corner and I'm lost. I didn't know I was going home until this morning. I'm confused, I'm scared, I'm frustrated, I'm depressed, and I don't know what's going to happen. I don't want to be a bad example to my friends and family, I don't even want to face them. This is all much harder than I ever imagined. If a mission is so good, why would the MTC be so horrible?"

4. In my office I sat across the room from a clean-cut, optimistic, intelligent student I had taught now for two semesters. After some small talk, tears began to well in his eyes. "I have dealt with same-sex attraction my entire life," he quietly began, looking down at the floor. "I didn't ask for this. I don't want this. I would give anything to be attracted to a woman, to live a normal life, to have feelings that other men feel. To get married. To have a family. I'd give anything to be able to follow the prophets. I study my scriptures every day. I pray. I attend the temple, I fast every week, I serve as much as I can, but these feelings won't leave me. My parents are pushing for me to get married, but they don't know what's happening in my heart. Why is this happening to me? I'm so angry."

5. "My husband gave me a blessing that everything would be okay with my pregnancy. I was so excited to be pregnant and start our new family. I don't understand how I could have such feelings of peace and hope, and been reassured by the priesthood blessing only to have my daughter pass away shortly after delivery."

After hearing these stories and many others, I have been humbled by their faith and conviction, especially as they answered my simple query: "So why are you staying?" I typically would explain to them that there are those who have been through difficult issues, have similar struggles, and so on, and it has caused those people to leave. "What then," I'd reiterate, "has caused you to stay?"

The girl that was raped gave an answer I couldn't believe. "Because even in the moment, I looked at the man's eyes and saw anger and evil, but I felt God's love. I knew He was aware of me even in this horrible moment. Now I realize that if it weren't for Heavenly Father, that man would have killed me that day. God saved my life." From the student who had just become aware of much more than he had ever known before about Joseph Smith came this reply to my query: "I've experienced so much and I know the Atonement of Jesus Christ is real. I couldn't imagine leaving over something so comparably insignificant." Why did the young woman who felt so demeaned as a woman in the Church stay? She explained, "Because even with all the questions I have and the struggles with women's issues, I feel that my relationship with my Heavenly Father is solid. Perhaps the members and even leaders of the Church struggle to reconcile women's issues, but I know where I stand with the Lord and I know how He sees women, and this is His Church, not mortals'." And so she stays.

The missionary who was dropped off at the side of the road and was struggling with depression and everything else—why does he stay? Because, in his simple words, "Jesus is my Savior. I went on my mission to serve Him. I'll stay for Him. He, of all people knows what it's like to feel abandoned." Why does the clean-cut returned missionary with same-sex attraction stay? "Because my attraction has nothing to do with my testimony. I admit that I'm angry at the Lord and that my situation doesn't make sense to me. I do know that Joseph Smith is a prophet, that he saw God and Jesus Christ. I do know the Book of Mormon is true. I believe that families are forever and I long for that. I'm not willing to give up my hopes and dreams and what I know to be true for what I know I do not understand even though it seems unfair and makes me angry. I have to trust that somehow, God's plan of happiness applies to me, too." And the young woman who lost her daughter following a priesthood blessing thoughtfully responded, "I know the world would have me be mad and deny the Church and the power of the priesthood. I recognize that God's ways are not my ways and His ways are higher than my ways. I've come to learn that not everything makes sense, but with time and patience, God makes all things right."

Sister Eliza R. Snow said: "I will smile at the rage of the tempest, and ride fearlessly and triumphantly across a boisterous ocean of circumstance. . . . And the *'testimony of Jesus'* will light up a lamp that will guide my vision through the portals of immortality."[2] What I've recognized with all of these individuals I've talked about is that, like Eliza R. Snow, they have all had extremely difficult circumstances. They have all had experiences which have led them to what I call the sweet spot, the point at which a decision has to be made. They have all been pressed to the very limit of where their testimony is, by a circumstance, typically not even a consequence of their choices, and they have to choose how to react. Others have been in similar circumstances and left. Why they stay, therefore, is not based on circumstance. It's based on character; it's based on the individual testimony and level of conversion; it's based on the price they've paid to come to know, come to understand, and come to be obedient to the teachings and the life of Jesus Christ. Somehow it seems that those who have stayed have built themselves upon the Rock of Jesus Christ. In other words, they are grounded.

Please understand that in so saying, I am not placing judgment on those who have chosen to leave. I believe there are as many reasons people leave as there are people. In answering the question, "Why would anyone leave?" President Dieter F. Uchtdorf replied, "Sometimes we assume it is because they have been offended or lazy or sinful. Actually, it is not that simple. In fact, there is not just one reason that applies to the variety of situations. Some of our dear members struggle for years with the question whether they should separate themselves from the Church. In this Church that honors personal agency so strongly, that was restored by a young man who asked questions and sought answers, we respect those who honestly search for truth. It may break our hearts when their journey takes them away from the Church we love and the truth we have found, but we honor their right to worship Almighty God according to the dictates of their own conscience, just as we claim that privilege for ourselves."[3]

Some of my dearest friends, family members, and close associates have strayed from or left the Church. I admit that it is painful to watch them go, and I would do literally anything to help them come back. In the meantime, I love them regardless. I have not walked in their shoes, experienced what they have experienced, or felt what they have felt. I am not here to judge. What I am talking about in this talk, however, is not about those who leave, but rather an observation regarding the character and attributes and actions of those who stay.

CONTINUALLY HOLDING

Perhaps one of the best known scriptural examples of a person who stayed strong in the Church even through times of great difficulty was Nephi. Although we may not know much about Nephi, we know that he lived during a time of great persecution, when the teachings of the Lord through the prophet, even his father, were enough to cause people, perhaps his own friends but for sure his brothers, to seek his life. We also know that he left his home, traveled in the wilderness for years, likely almost starved to death, carried upon himself the burden of not only providing for himself, but also his wife, likely children, and extended family. He boarded a boat to an unknown place, lost both of his parents upon arrival to an unknown land, and more. It is difficult to know how much his faith was challenged, but it doesn't take much imagination to recognize the possibility. By studying just the first few chapters of Nephi, we are able to recognize some of his sweet spots and how he responded.

He, like his older brothers, had been taught and asked to do things that were troubling and difficult to understand. Unlike his brethren, however, who "murmur[ed] because they knew not the dealings of that God who had created them" (1 Nephi 2:12), Nephi took responsibility for his lack of knowledge and understanding and "did cry unto the Lord; and behold he did visit me, and did soften my heart that I did believe all the words which had been spoken by my father; wherefore, I did not rebel against him like unto my brothers" (v. 16). Later, after their first unsuccessful attempt to obtain the plates of brass as had been commanded by the Lord, Nephi admits that he and his brethren were "exceedingly sorrowful" (1 Nephi 16:20). Nephi, unlike his brethren, however, during yet another sweet spot experience, refuses to allow this sorrow to halt their progress. He declared, "As the Lord liveth, and as we live, we will not go down unto our father in the wilderness until we have accomplished the thing which the Lord hath commanded us" (1 Nephi 3:15). Nephi could have easily blamed the Lord for not keeping his promise, but rather, Nephi, knowing the will of the Lord and having had it confirmed in his heart, forges forward and convinces his brethren, through reason, to try again. After the second failed attempt, however, Nephi was on his own, being "led by the Spirit, not knowing beforehand the things which I should do. Nevertheless, I went forth" (1 Nephi 4:6–7).

Perhaps the greatest test of his faith came after being led by the Spirit to find Laban and being "constrained by the Spirit" (1 Nephi 4:10) to now kill him. Although there is much we do not know about Nephi's life and experiences, one thing we do know at this point is that Nephi has paid the price to understand the voice of the Spirit. He does not kill Laban because he does not see; rather, he kills Laban because he does see the big picture. With a narrower view, Nephi perhaps would have been more sympathetic to Laban; he may have perhaps let him live, but in so doing he would have not only been disobedient to the Spirit, but he would have been the cause of the ignorance of his father's posterity. Nephi understood the importance of the plates, the record which taught the truths of salvation, and so he went forth again and "did obey the voice of the Spirit" (v. 18).

It is not surprising for the reader, then, to see Nephi, after his father related his sacred dream unto him and his brothers, desiring to "see, and hear, and know of these things, by the power of the Holy Ghost" for himself (1 Nephi 10:17). For, he explains, the Holy Ghost "is the gift of God unto all those who diligently seek him [the Messiah], as well in times of old as in the time that he should manifest himself unto the children of men . . . For he that diligently seeketh shall find; and the mysteries of God shall be unfolded unto them, by the power of the Holy Ghost, as well in these times as in times of old, and as well in times of old as in times to come; wherefore, the course of the Lord is one eternal round" (1 Nephi 10:17, 19).

Although Nephi trusted in his father, Lehi, and believed he was a prophet and had already proved his obedience, he also recognized the importance of his own spiritual self-reliance. He desired to know, understand, and be converted himself. Clearly Nephi wanted more than information, more than knowledge— he wanted to be grounded in the teachings of his father, and more important, in the teachings of the Lord. It seems that he had come to recognize the critical role of the Spirit in understanding and conversion. Just like Joseph Smith, he wasn't willing to settle, to stop short. Like Joseph Smith, Nephi acknowledged his lack of wisdom and went to the Lord for answers. Both were willing to put the Lord to the test and act in obedience upon the direction given. Both proved themselves worthy through obedience to the Spirit and the word of God to receive answers to heartfelt questions and pushed through adversarial afflictions to receive direction. Neither Joseph nor Nephi were settled with answers given by mortals; they both sought confirmation from the Lord and the Spirit and therefore became spiritually self-reliant in the process.

So in this story of Lehi's dream, what Lehi saw in regard to Nephi in comparison to Laman and Lemuel is no surprise. After describing the fruit of the tree that he ate, which was "desirable to make one happy" and "white, to exceed all the whiteness I had ever seen," Lehi declares that the fruit did fill "my soul with exceedingly great joy," and therefore, he "began to be desirous that my family should partake of it also." (1 Nephi 8:10–12). In trying to draw his family unto him, Lehi described three groups of people "pressing forward, that they might obtain the path which led unto the tree" (v.21). All of those he saw encountered a "mist of darkness" (v.23), but each group reacted differently.

All Lehi tells us about the first group is that upon encountering the mist of darkness they "did lose their way, that they wandered off and were lost" (1 Nephi 8:23). There is no mention of an iron rod with them, or of scriptures or the word of God. It seems that that they had nothing to hold onto, therefore they had no direction, and they simply fell away. That's all we know; they fall away.

The second group of people "caught hold of the end of the rod of iron; and they did press forward through the mist of darkness, clinging to the rod of iron, even until they did come forth and partake of the fruit of the tree" (1 Nephi 8:24). Elder Bednar explains that *clinging* seems to imply "occasional '*bursts*' of study or irregular dipping rather than consistent, ongoing immersion in the word of God."[4] Frankly, I think this is the case with many of us. Perhaps during the more difficult times we study our scriptures, pray, fast, wrestle, but then when life gets easy or busy—or we simply get lazy or become distracted by a myriad of other good, but not as important things—we too quickly let go. This is the scary group because clearly they know that the iron rod is there; clearly they feel like they should be holding on, but there are so many distractions, whatever they are, that cause them to let go. Elder Richard G. Scott inquired of the members of the Church,

"Are there so many fascinating, exciting things to do or so many challenges pressing down upon you that it is hard to keep focused on that which is essential?" He then taught, "When things of the world crowd in, all too often the wrong things take highest priority. Then it is easy to forget the fundamental purpose of life. Satan has a powerful tool to use against good people. It is distraction. He would have good people fill life with 'good things' so there is no room for the essential ones." Then, inviting us to self-evaluate he simply asks, "Have you unconsciously been caught in that trap?"[5]

The result of these distractions or skewed priorities is clearly taught in the story of the wise and foolish man. The wise man builds his house upon the rock. The rock is Christ. The foolish man builds his house upon the sand. What is the sand? Anything *but* Christ. As it says in Helaman 5:12, the winds and the waves start blowing and the person who builds his house on the rock "cannot fall." The winds and the waves clearly include all of the distractions that are beating us down. Whatever that distraction is: whether it's fear, whether it's jealousy, whether it's money, whether it's divorce, whatever emotional problem, whether it's losing a job, having a miscarriage, being single, it doesn't matter. Whatever it is, if it is causing someone to leave Christ, or build their foundation on something else, it is a distraction. So then what happens to these people? They partake of the fruit of the tree, but "did cast their eyes about," saw the mocking of those in the great and spacious building, and "they fell away into forbidden paths and were lost" (1 Nephi 8:25, 28).

The third group, however, "caught hold of the end of the rod of iron; and they did press their way forward, continually holding fast to the rod of iron, until they came forth and fell down and partook of the fruit of the tree" (1 Nephi 8:30). They too noticed pointing fingers of scorn from the multitude who had entered the great and spacious building, "but we heeded them not" (v. 33). Unlike the second group who partook and fell away, the third group "came forth and fell down and partook of the fruit of the tree" (v. 30). Or, in other words, they fell at the feet of Christ.

So it seems that the only critical point between the first and second group is that one "clings" and the other "continually holds." Why does continually holding lead someone to not fall away? I believe it is simply this: those who "continually hold" show they are willing to pay the price at whatever cost. They paid the price in that they studied; they paid the price in that they didn't let go; they were paying the price in that they were being obedient to the Lord. And the more obedient to the Lord they were, and the more they applied the gospel of Jesus Christ in their lives, and the more they studied the life of Christ, the more they knew Christ. So when they got to the tree, unlike the other group, they fell down because they knew Him, because they reverenced Him, because they respected Him, because they knew what He had done for them. This group didn't stand or kneel, but rather, they fell and never left.

FALLING AT HIS FEET AND RECEIVING HIS POWER

President Russell M. Nelson, in the April 2017 general conference, explained a pattern to receiving God's power: "The more we know about the Savior's ministry and mission—the more we understand His doctrine and what He did for us—the more we know that He can provide the power that we need for our lives." Then, as we act upon that knowledge, especially regarding the Savior's atoning sacrifice and His character, "we choose to have faith in Him and follow Him." That faith then motivates to more action and gives us even "more access to His power."[6]

I have absolutely no question that the more we learn about Christ and strive to draw close to Him and the more we become like Him, the more likely we are to fall at His feet. And the further we stray from Christ, for whatever reason, and the more we concern ourselves with things that are not important, the more likely we are to fall away from Him.

I love this true principle shared by Elder Dale G. Renlund in general conference: "'The greater the distance between the giver and the receiver, the more the receiver develops a sense of entitlement.' . . . The closer we are to Jesus Christ in the thoughts and intents of our hearts, the more we appreciate His innocent suffering, the more grateful we are for grace and forgiveness, and the more we want to repent and become like Him."[7] Using this principle it is easy to see why those who hold continually fall at the feet of Christ—and those who cling to the rod, or never even acknowledge it, are more likely to leave.

Note this phrase that Elder Renlund uses that he attributes to Elder Wilford W. Andersen of the Seventy: *The greater the distance between the giver and the receiver, the more the receiver develops a sense of entitlement.* Those who desire the great and spacious building over Christ cannot possibly understand what they are giving up. They haven't paid the price to know. They don't understand that what they have right there in their hand is more important and more valuable and more grandiose than anything that anyone else could ever possibly give them—because they haven't paid the price to recognize what the tree is yet, they are willing to go somewhere else. The great paradox in some cases is simply that at first they blame God for what they did not receive and eventually, some then deny His very existence.

I absolutely have no question that with maybe a rare exception, people who know Christ and who have paid the price to know Christ will never fall away. They wouldn't. They couldn't. They are desperate for Him. They have come to understand, perhaps from those clinging moments in their lives when they let go from time to time, nothing else is good enough. Nothing else really compares.

In this process of drawing closer to Christ I believe it is critical to remember that no one is perfect. There may be times in our lives when we figuratively "let go." The key is to stop letting go as much as we possibly can and for shorter periods of time and to ask for forgiveness as we repent and move forward. There is a difference between divine discontent and what I would term demonic despondency. Divine discontent is a healthy result of our knowledge of our divine nature coupled with the acknowledgment of our individual imperfections and thus a desire to improve. Demonic despondency is the feeling of worthlessness, of giving up. Divine discontent draws us upward; demonic despondency beats us down.

TRUNK, BRANCHES, AND LEAVES

I hope it's obvious that we want to be among those who are continually holding to the iron rod and who fall at the feet of Christ. We want to be among the group that is grounded, firmly planted on the rock of Christ. Our leaders are depending on us and pleading with us to do so. Elder M. Russell Ballard urged us forward as he declared:

"We need the women of the Church to know the doctrine of Christ. . . . Never has there been a more complex time in the history of the earth. Satan and his minions have been perfecting the weapons in their arsenal for millennia, and they are experienced at destroying faith and trust in God and in the Lord Jesus Christ among the human family. . . . We need more of the distinctive, influential voices and faith of women. We need you to learn the doctrine and to understand what we believe so that you can bear your testimonies about the truth of all things. . . . Only you can show the world what women of God who have made covenants look like and believe."[8]

Notice the focus: understand the doctrine of Christ. More recently, President Russell M. Nelson's inspiring "Plea to the Sisters" that so many of us loved, prophesied that "attacks against the Church, its doctrine, and our way of life are going to increase." He then exhorted, "Because of this, we need women who have a bedrock understanding of the doctrine of Christ and who will use that understanding to teach and to help raise a sin-resistant generation."[9] In Sister Linda K. Burton's first general conference address as the Relief Society General President of the Church, she declared, "We have felt that Heavenly Father would first have us help His beloved daughters understand the doctrine of the Atonement of Jesus Christ."[10]

Perhaps this diagram can help individuals comprehend why knowing and understanding the doctrine of Christ is so critical and how being able to distinguish the doctrines and principles of the gospel from the applications/policies/rules/practices and actions is so critical.

Notice that on this tree, the trunk is the doctrine—the saving doctrines of the gospel of Jesus Christ. Elder David A. Bednar defined "a gospel doctrine" as "a truth—a truth of salvation revealed by a loving heavenly Father." He continues, "Gospel doctrines are eternal, do not change, and pertain to the eternal progression and exaltation of Heavenly Father's sons and daughters. Doctrines such as the nature of the Godhead, the plan of happiness, and the Atonement of Jesus Christ are foundational, fundamental, and comprehensive."[11]

The branches on the tree represent principles. Elder Bednar states that "a *gospel principle* is a doctrinally based guideline for the righteous exercise of moral agency."[12] Correct principles of the gospel are connected to and derive from saving doctrines of the gospel of Jesus Christ. True principles do not change. They provide direction and give guidelines for proper behavior and action.

Elder Richard G. Scott explained, "Principles are concentrated truth, packaged for application to a wide variety of circumstances. A true principle makes decisions clear even under the most confusing and compelling circumstances. It is worth great effort to organize the truth we gather to simple statements of principle."[13]

Very rarely do I see members of the Church get upset over doctrines and principles of the gospel of Jesus Christ. Very few members are willing to leave the Church over the doctrine of the Atonement of Christ, the priesthood, or the plan of salvation. Very few, if any, are upset and willing to leave the Church over the principles of receiving revelation, the importance of obedience, the need to repent and forgive, to exercise more faith, or to improve one's ability to practice Christlike charity. In fact, most members love these doctrines and principles and have strong testimonies of them and most others. It is not typically the trunk and branches—or in other words, the doctrines and principles—that are difficult. The leaves, however, can be another story.

The leaves are the applications, policies, rules, actions, practices, and procedures that derive from principles and doctrines. "Applications [rules, actions, practices, and procedures]," according to Elder Bednar, "appropriately can vary according to needs and circumstances."[14] For example, obedience and revelation are principles of the gospel of Jesus Christ tied directly to saving doctrine. God has given revelation to and expected obedience from all of his prophets from Adam to President Monson. The specific revelation and the required obedience to that command, however, are not always the same. God gave revelation to Joseph Smith, for example, and expected him to obey. But God's revelation to Joseph Smith did not command him to build an ark or to kill Laban.

Some of the leaves on the tree can be extremely difficult and often come without explanation. Examples of leaves on the tree that are often difficult include policy changes that oppose personal values, a historical issue that may not have been explained well previously or understood correctly, a word of offense from a ward member, an unanswered blessing, and/or a seemingly unexpected or unfair hardship or adversity. These leaves are all real and can affect us all at different times for various reasons.

I have found that those people who pay the price to know and live the foundational saving doctrines and principles of the gospel of Jesus Christ are better able to make sense of and deal with the leaves. In other words, those who focus on Christ and His doctrine and principles are more capable of discerning truth, of seeing clearly and putting things into proper eternal perspective. The Prophet Joseph Smith exclaimed: "The fundamental principles of our religion are the testimony of the Apostles and Prophets, concerning Jesus Christ, that He died, was buried, and rose again the third day, and ascended into heaven; and all other things which pertain to our religion are only appendages to it."[15]

That does not mean that we are unaffected *by* the leaves, nor does it mean that we always understand the reasons *for* the leaves. What it does mean is that we see the leaves for what they are and are able to put them in proper perspective. Those who can differentiate between the saving doctrines and associated principles from applications, practices, principles, or rules are typically more grounded. They know in whom they have trusted and they wouldn't leave over a leaf. They wouldn't. They couldn't. They recognize how much they would lose over "a mess of pottage" (see Genesis 25:29–34).

As Elder Jeffrey R. Holland emotionally inquired of Church Educational System teachers worldwide, "What conceivable historical or doctrinal or procedural issue that may arise among any group could ever overshadow or negate one's consuming spiritual conviction regarding the Father's merciful plan of salvation; His

Only Begotten Son's birth, mission, Atonement, and Resurrection; the reality of the First Vision; the restoration of the priesthood; the receipt of divine revelation, both personally and institutionally; the soul-shaping spirit and moving power of the Book of Mormon; the awe and majesty of the temple endowment; one's own personal experience with true miracles; and on and on and on?" He continues, "It is a mystery to me how those majestic, eternal, first-level truths [doctrines] so central to the grandeur of the *whole* gospel message can be set aside or completely dismissed by some in favor of obsessing over second- or third- or fourth-level pieces [leaves] of that whole. To me, this is, in words attributed to Edith Wharton, truly being trapped in 'the thick of thin things.'"[16]

PAYING THE PRICE

I believe it is the same with us. If we want to make sure we and our families don't get trapped in the "thick of thin things," we must make sure we stay focused on those things that are substantial and significant, even crucial. We must know and teach the doctrines and principles of the gospel of Jesus Christ. If we want to ensure that we and our families never forget the Savior, we must do all we can to remember Him, to build upon Him. We must keep Him at the forefront of our lives. We have pictures of Him on our walls; we study the scriptures; we attend the temple; we learn of Him and His doctrine by studying and memorizing the scriptures and words of the prophets, including "The Living Christ,"[17] and by applying His principles and teachings and following His example; we make and keep sacred covenants, including worthily participating in the sacrament weekly—we make Him important in our lives. We pray to the Father in the name of Jesus Christ, trying to align our will with His. As President Nelson so poignantly taught from personal experience:

"There is nothing easy or automatic about becoming such powerful disciples. Our focus must be riveted on the Savior and His gospel. It is mentally rigorous to strive to look unto Him in *every* thought. But when we do, our doubts and fears flee."[18]

So we make Jesus Christ the center of everything. "We talk of Christ, we rejoice in Christ, we preach of Christ, we prophesy of Christ, and we write according to our prophecies, that our children may know to what source they may look for a remission of their sins" (2 Nephi 25:26).

But a warning—reading scriptures and saying prayers and going to the temple is a good start, but if we are doing it to mark it off of our to-do list, we are likely missing the point. I can't tell you how many times I've said my prayer and I've gotten up to leave and I couldn't remember if I'd just prayed or not. Have you done that? I mean, two minutes later and I'm running out the door wondering if I remembered to pray. Incredible! What is that telling me about my prayer? Is it possible if I'm praying like that that maybe I'm not focusing on Jesus Christ or His Atonement? Maybe I'm not really praying, but rather just going through the motions to check it off. What is that showing the Lord? What kind of entitlement am I feeling? How in the world do I know if the Lord is answering my prayers if I don't even know what I prayed for? How do I know if I'm acting in faith if I didn't even pay attention to what the Spirit guided me to do in response to my prayer or scripture study? President Henry B. Eyring taught that "the effect of sincere prayer and of careful scripture study is to always feel an urging to do things."[19] If we can sincerely say that we are praying and studying our scriptures, but aren't receiving an answer to a prayer or receiving the guidance or help that we need, perhaps we need to pay attention to and improve our praying and scripture study.

President Gordon B. Hinckley told CES teachers to teach their students "how to pray."[20] He was talking to teachers whose students were all members of the Church. We don't need to just pray to check it off—we need to pray to come to Christ. We need to repent to come to Christ. We need to pray and apply Christ's Atonement in our lives.

In his April 2017 general conference address, President Thomas S. Monson spoke for a little over three minutes. As part of his short message, he related the following: "We live in a time of great trouble and wickedness. What will protect us from the sin and the evil so prevalent in the world today? I maintain that a strong testimony of our Savior, Jesus Christ, and of His gospel will help see us through to safety." I remember asking my students the following Monday what President Monson's talk was about. Without fail, the students said that his talk was on the Book of Mormon. They were right. President Monson continued, "If you are not reading the Book of Mormon each day, please do so."[21] But is it possible that we missed the *why* behind reading the Book of Mormon? He's asking us to read the Book of Mormon because he wants us to have a strong testimony of our Savior, Jesus Christ, and His gospel so that we can be safe. That's his focus. His focus is on the doctrine of Christ and His Atonement—the principle is that if you read the Book of Mormon you will better understand the doctrine of Jesus Christ and be safe. You will become like Him and therefore you'll be protected from the sin and evil that is so prevalent in the world. The focus is on Christ. This is critical.

In spiritual things, it is so easy to confuse the means with the end. When I taught seminary, I used to have students raise their hands if they'd read their scriptures. I calculated the percentage and kept a daily record on the board for each class. Looking back,

I'm sure I was the direct cause of many students feeling good and guilty. I was probably the cause of some of them even lying just to look good. I didn't mean to, but I'm sure that's what I did. In retrospect, I wish I would have just asked, "Who here drew closer to Christ yesterday in your scripture study . . . and would you please share?" Can you see what a difference just changing this one question could make? We can ask ourselves similar questions in our own scripture study. "How did I draw closer to Christ in my scripture study?" "What is the Spirit guiding me to do as a result of my prayer and scripture study?" I believe if we focus on Christ better we will be more likely to build our own testimony and help others find and strengthen their own. Asking the right questions is a part of the stretching process.

President Nelson recently talked about stretching. In reference to the woman with the issue of blood he instructed: "This faithful, focused women needed to stretch as far as she could to access His power. Her physical stretching was symbolic of her spiritual stretching. . . . When you reach up for the Lord's power in your life with the same intensity that a drowning person has when grasping and gasping for air, power from Jesus Christ will be yours. When the Savior knows that you truly want to reach up to Him—when He can feel that the greatest desire of your heart is to draw His power into your life—you will be led by the Holy Ghost to know exactly what you should do."[22] The Savior himself understands what it means to stretch. As Elder Neal A. Maxwell so eloquently related, "Jesus' brief stumbling while carrying the cross is a reminder as to how close to the very edge of our strength God stretches us at times."[23]

We don't have to be drowning to recognize our dependence on air. A knowledge of who the Savior is through continually holding to the rod will help us, like Nephi, better understand our complete dependence on Him. Are we not all beggars? I know that I am a desperate beggar, but I recognize that at times I am often not stretching enough, am not "continually holding," or am not building on the rock. I do, however, know that when I gasp for air and when I am doing my best to "continually hold," and when I am building on the Rock of Christ, He is always there. Always. He has yet to fail me.

CONCLUSION

In his "Plea to My Sisters," President Nelson declared, "My dear sisters, nothing is more crucial to your eternal life than your own conversion."[24] I testify that Jesus is the Christ, that He desires that we learn His doctrine and come unto Him. I testify that Satan is trying to destroy us as women, but God has set bounds even on Satan. If you want to make sure that you don't fall, build upon the rock of the Redeemer. As it says in the Book of Mormon, "Can a women forget her sucking child, that she should not have compassion on the son of her womb? Yea, they may forget, yet will I not forget thee, O house of Israel. Behold, I have graven thee upon the palms of my hands; thy walls are continually before me" (1 Nephi 21:15–16). The key is to have His image engraven upon our countenances. It's hard to forget Christ when you look in the mirror and that's what you see. I testify that Jesus is the Christ. I also testify that everything we do, whatever it takes, every stretch is worth it.

BECOMING A CONVERTED, COVENANT-KEEPING WOMAN

Neill F. Marriott

I hope, for the next few minutes, we can consider the power of God that is available to each one of us. This power is ours to have, if we want it. It is our privilege to live with it and act with it and become more like the Savior with it.

What is this power? It is the power that comes from faithful participation in gospel ordinances and covenants. "An ordinance is a sacred, formal act performed by the authority of the priesthood."[1]

A converted woman is connected to godly power through participating in ordinances and keeping covenants. Sisters, as we consider this power, please keep the word "yoked" in your heart and mind.

Do you know what it is like to be without covenants which yoke us to the Lord—to be without the trusted guidance of the Spirit and the direction of the covenant path? Let me tell you how it feels.

When I was fifteen years old my parents and I attended an Easter revival service at our Protestant church in Louisiana. We had a guest minister who gave a sermon, which I don't remember,

and then introduced the last hymn, entitled "Just as I Am"—
which I do vividly remember. The first verse goes:

> *Just as I am, without one plea,*
> *But that Thy blood was shed for me,*
> *And that Thou bid'st me come to Thee,*
> *O Lamb of God, I come! I come!*[2]

Each of the five verses ends with the words "O Lamb of God,
I come! I come!"

As I sang, the tears began to well up. I wanted to come unto
Christ. Our minister stopped the hymn momentarily and invited
any and all to come down to the altar as we sang the last verse,
to witness that we were coming to Christ. So as the last verse was
being sung, several members of our congregation began to slowly
walk down to the altar railing. I walked to the altar too.

When the hymn ended, we milled around for a moment. The
minister heartily shook our hands and then my parents and I
went home. *Was that it?* I thought. *Did I come to Christ?* It felt
like I had only gotten as far as the altar.

2 Timothy 3:5 speaks of men in the last days "having a form
of godliness, but denying the power thereof." The Savior Himself
spoke these words to Joseph Smith in the First Vision, describing
the religious leaders of the day as "having a form of godliness, but
they deny the power thereof" (Joseph Smith–History 1:19).

What did our good minister lack at the Easter revival meeting? He did have a form of godliness and was probably a good
Christian man, but he had no authority to offer the Lord's priesthood ordinances to me.

When we participate humbly and obediently in saving

ordinances we are turning to God, we are *yoked* to the Savior and can then receive His power in our lives.

These words sound rather normal to us, don't they? Ordinances and covenants. . . . Do we take them and the accompanying power lightly? If so, we, as Brigham Young said, are living "beneath our privileges."[3]

And we want those privileges! A few of them are:

- The privilege of being secure and confident in knowing and living what is true and lasting when all around us are the changeable, partial truths of the world.
- The privilege of knowing we are loved and valued even when we may be abused, ignored, or taken for granted by others.
- The privilege of being emotionally strengthened, healed, and guided by the Holy Ghost because of the Savior's Atonement.
- The privilege of spiritual clarity to identify Satan's temptations.
- The privilege of spiritual strength to turn from those temptations.
- The privilege of serving others with inspiration from the Holy Ghost.
- The privilege of being yoked to the Savior Jesus Christ, feeling His grace and mercy abiding with us and being thus empowered to serve as He would have us serve.

These gospel privileges come when we, as converted disciples of Christ, make and keep sacred *covenants*.

I am thinking almost all of us have made sacred covenants. But the making of covenants will be an empty gesture if we stop there. It is the understanding of, the application of, and the keeping of our promises to the Lord that generate a flow of covenant privileges into our daily lives.

Now, we are fallen creatures, we know this. And on this earth we will experience the suffering that comes with mortal life. There are two kinds of suffering, in my opinion. One is useful to us, as Orson F. Whitney wrote, "All that we suffer and all that we endure, especially when we endure it patiently, builds up our characters, purifies our hearts, expands our souls, and makes us more tender and charitable, more worthy to be called the children of God."[4]

We are here to experience both the blessings and the difficulties of mortality; these trials are our dear tutors which stretch our capacity to depend on Jesus Christ and His Atonement for us. When a trial comes, let it be a prompting to *convert* our thoughts and efforts to Christ, to yoke ourselves to Him, and feel the beautiful power that comes from keeping covenants and doing His work.

Throughout our life, and especially during trials, gospel ordinances can open the door to strength beyond our own and to greater knowledge of God Himself. Knowing the Lord better, we are enabled to become more like Him. This "becoming" process requires patient diligence and will turn good women into Christlike women. This turning process is conversion.

We have covenanted to comfort those that stand in need of comfort and I daresay that everyone needs some kind of comfort this very minute! I do.

Who will you comfort today, with a heart made tender by the influence of your baptismal covenant and the gift of the Holy Ghost? Will you be sensitive to someone's feelings who needs to feel valuable, included, or reassured? I remember sitting alone at a table in the Wilkinson Center at this very conference in 2014. A sister sat down by me and offered me some of her mint brownie. I immediately felt warmed by her extended friendship. And very happy with that brownie, too! We can reach out sensitively every single day to warm someone's heart.

Usually the one who stands in need of your comfort is the one that feels like your biggest bother! As you pray for help with all energy of heart to love this person, you'll naturally begin to draw closer to the Spirit. Because Heavenly Father loves you personally, and because you asked for help, He will bestow a portion of His love upon you and you can begin to offer goodness to the one who has been difficult for you to love. Studying Moroni 7:48 will give you keys to wisdom about this relationship.

Aside from tribulations that teach us to come unto Christ, there is another kind of suffering. It is *needless suffering*. It is willfully choosing the way of the world when we know God's way is the right way. Elder D. Todd Christofferson said, "[Heavenly Father] is a tender parent who would spare us needless suffering and grief and at the same time help us realize our divine potential."[5]

Have faith in this truth: You have help available for every problem! Reach for it. The Lord will not leave us comfortless. As we make and keep covenants by participating in ordinances, we can understand His will and act on it. We will be given more and more strength to come through trials. And we can even do it cheerfully.

Take the cases of the people of Alma and the people of Limhi. One group had made covenants with the Lord, one had not. The difference in their suffering shows the power of ordinances and covenants. Remember, both of these groups were surrounded by Lamanites and danger. Both had huge trials facing them.

We read about the people of Limhi, many of whom had rejected the words of the prophet Abinadi, and thus were left with only their own mortal strength. In Mosiah 21 we read that they put on their armor and went forth against the Lamanites to drive them out of their land three times—and the Lamanites beat them every time. They were on their own in battle and were defeated. How often do we put on our makeup and go out to face the day only on our own power? The challenges of mortality will eventually beat us down into unhappiness if the Lord's power is missing in our lives.

The people of Limhi suffered needlessly! After being defeated and broken in battle they were in bondage; they cried to the Lord to deliver them. What was the Lord's response? Mosiah 21:15 states, "And now the Lord was slow to hear their cry because of their iniquities."

Eventually the Lord did soften the hearts of the Lamanites so the burdens were eased but the Lord didn't see fit to immediately deliver them out of bondage. Without the blessings connected to making and keeping covenants, Limhi and his people were unable to enjoy the full covenant blessings. Eventually they were converted and Alma did baptize them, and then the Lord did pour out His Spirit upon them.

Do we act as these people of Limhi? Do we try and try again to solve a challenge in our life and get defeated time and again? Are we trying to conquer these on our own without relying on the power from Heavenly Father that comes with sacred covenants? The Lord holds out the reassurance of His grace and power to all His covenant-keeping daughters! The empowering influence of the temple, the sacrament, prayer, the scriptures, the Holy Ghost, and much more are ours as we are converted to Him.

On the other hand, consider the power of the followers of Alma the Younger after they chose to be baptized and entered into a covenant with the Lord. Ordinances unify man with God; thus yoked to eternal power, Alma's people in adversity had much divine help that Limhi's people lacked.

Look at their blessings, though attacked on all sides:

1. Alma and his people were warned about the approaching armies of King Noah and they escaped.
2. The Lord strengthened them that the armies couldn't overtake them.
3. When they were in bondage to the Lamanites, they prayed with all their hearts and the Lord said:
   - Lift up your heads and be of good comfort, for I know of the covenant which ye have made unto me,
   - And I will covenant with my people and deliver them out of bondage.
   - And I will also ease the burdens which are put upon your shoulders that even you cannot feel them upon your backs . . .
4. The Lord strengthened them that they could carry the burden with ease and they became cheerful and patient to the will of the Lord.
5. Finally their faith became so great that the Lord guided them to safety.

Do you identify with the people of Limhi or the people of Alma? Are you fighting a losing battle with troubles or are you applying your faith in hard situations and drawing the strength that comes from keeping covenants? Let's not live beneath the privilege of receiving God's help.

The privileges of the covenant only come alive for us when we are *converted* to the gospel of Jesus Christ. The Latin root of the word *convert* means to turn again. This "turning" is a beautiful way to express how we change our heart and come unto the Savior.

If you were to press me on this point of how to be converted, I would say that earnest prayer and questions like "What does Heavenly Father want me to do? What do I need to change about myself?" begin a change in our hearts. If asked honestly, we will receive an answer as we continue to listen.

After about six months of studying the Church, I honestly prayed to know if the Church was true. I promised Father in Heaven I would act on His answer to my question. I meant it. I asked simply, "I need to know if this is the only true church of Jesus Christ on the earth and if it is, I'll be baptized." I *felt* the answer "It is true" as though words were spoken. My heart did turn at that moment to God and my joy bubbled up instantly. Your simple honest prayers will turn you again to God. That is a step in conversion.

Now (and I shared this prayer process twenty years ago at BYU Women's Conference), I sometimes prepare to talk with Heavenly Father by doing several things:

1. I go where I can be completely alone and not be interrupted (when the kids were little I would lock the bedroom door and sometimes, after praying, I would find hot dogs pushed under the door!)
2. I kneel down. I've learned that when I make my body be reverent, more reverent thoughts follow.
3. I visualize Heavenly Father standing in front of me,

above me and looking down, smiling—after all, I want to direct my words toward Him.

4. Next, I pray aloud. (I've learned that when I pray in my mind my thoughts will wander and I end up telling Heavenly Father things like the price of gasoline.)

5. Then I pour out my heart to Him in private prayer, just the two of us, expressing my feelings for Him. I think of it as bearing my testimony to my eternal Father. I testify to Him of the things I know about Him.

6. After that, I just offer what's in my heart, the deep questions, the good and the bad mixed together—what should I change in myself, am I holding back anything? Do I give my all to His will? I plead for answers and sometimes the response is so simple it would be easy to dismiss—like "Turn off the radio and pray while driving to the store." We've got to listen after we pray!

Another way to "turn again" and be converted is to open the scriptures and read. When I was expecting our tenth baby it was a hot, hot summer. Our home didn't have air conditioning and I always felt exhausted. (I even fell asleep in the chair at the grocery store pharmacy as I waited for a prescription! A nice neighbor woke me up.) I found that relief came, not by sitting in front of the fan, but by opening the Book of Mormon. Sometimes I was too weary to even read, so I just closed my eyes and hugged that Book of Mormon to my chest. Maybe that's a loose interpretation of "feeling" the truth of the Book of Mormon.

Opening the scriptures humbly is an act of faith. I feel like it sends a signal to heaven—"Look, she's opened her scriptures, she wants to know more about the Lord!" Surely such action alerts the Spirit! Occasionally our hearts may not be humble—but open the scriptures anyway. Something good will come of it, especially if you read with a pen and journal to write impressions you receive.

Reading scriptures regularly has—bit by bit—given me revelation about what needs to change in my heart and has shown me solutions to long-standing problems. Continue on, praying for and seeking for the answers in the scriptures.

I can't talk about converting power without speaking of the temple. There is light and truth inside these sacred edifices for each who enters that can be found nowhere else on earth. To turn to the Lord, go to the temple, go prayerfully and meekly.

Through participation in sacred temple ordinances we come to know God, and then we are irresistibly drawn to His love and our conversion increases. In the temple you will connect to heaven as you offer the eternal ordinances to a waiting, deceased, oh-so-grateful sister who can then progress in her own conversion.

President Russell M. Nelson taught us: "We . . . increase the Savior's power in our lives when we make sacred covenants and keep those covenants with precision. Our covenants bind us to Him and give us godly power."[6] What is the difference between an endowed LDS sister, absorbed in her troubles, who forgets to "always remember Him" and a sister who has strength in affliction, hope in dark times, and love for others?

I have been both of these sisters and I believe the difference lies in whether or not we follow President Russell M. Nelson's counsel to bind ourselves by covenant to the Lord. Jesus Christ invites us to be yoked to him (see Matthew 11:29) and that yoking is done by daily living the covenants we make.

On the eve of the Savior's crucifixion, as the Apostles sat with the Lord at the Last Supper, Peter, the head of the Twelve, declared that he would lay down his life for the Christ. The Savior tenderly but directly replied, "Simon, Simon, . . . when thou are converted, strengthen thy brethren" (Luke 22:31–32).

Knowing that even after three years with the Savior, Peter was still in the process of being converted tells me that we can all continue to grow in our conversion and strengthen our sisters.

Lyrics to a hymn by Charles Wesley say:

> *A charge to keep I have,*
> *A God to glorify,*
> *A never-dying soul to save,*
> *And fit it for the sky.*
> *To serve the present age,*
> *My calling to fulfill:*
> *Oh, may it all my pow'rs engage*
> *To do my Master's will!*[7]

Notice the wisdom and inspiration in the words. First, we have a responsibility to fit our own never-dying souls for heaven. And once we are working on that, we have a calling in our present circumstance to serve others according to the Master's will.

So what does a converted, covenant-keeping woman do?

When our lovely twenty-one-year-old daughter was hit by a truck, my husband and I and three of our children were in Brazil serving a mission. All of the children living in the United States flew immediately to the Indiana hospital where Georgia lay, fighting for her life. The ones staying in our home, understandably, left the house in great disarray as they rushed to find a plane. Dear neighbors spoke to one another about the situation and the next morning, as the family was in Indiana trying to cope with Georgia's passing, twenty-five covenant-keeping sisters gathered at our home in Salt Lake City.

TEACHING IN THE SAVIOR'S WAY

Camille Fronk Olson

Those of us with teaching callings in the Church have been exploring "Teaching in the Savior's Way" almost every month in our ward teacher councils. What a remarkable program this is: time set aside to encourage us to share ideas and explore teaching practices and principles that the Savior utilized so well. Because of the current ward program, I purposely chose not to draw from the *Teaching in the Savior's Way* manual produced by the Church. Rather, I am focusing on what made Jesus such a remarkable teacher from what I have discovered through scripture study. I am in awe of His ability to communicate and elicit change in His "students." I hope to identify a few principles that may be helpful or meaningful for us to consider and supplement the foundational objectives outlined in the manual.

As a basis for our appreciation of Jesus's example, we cannot simply see the Savior as a great teacher. He is so much more than that. Consider a statement from President J. Reuben Clark Jr., a member of the First Presidency from 1934–61: "It's all right to speak about the Savior and the beauty of His doctrines and the beauty of truth. But this is the thing I wish you to always

They came in the front door with their cleaning supplies, buckets, and brooms. Whispering to one another, they chose different parts of our disheveled home and began the work of angels. For several hours they served quietly. Sometimes, as Janene, a neighbor, said, they wept as they worked. Some weeded the front flower beds and planted fresh flowers around the doorstep. Others scrubbed the kitchen, dusted and polished furniture, cleaned floors, and shined windows. When the work was finished, they gathered just as quietly in our living room. This covenant-keeping circle of friends knelt together, united their faith, and prayed that there would be a blessing on our home and family—that we would feel peace and love as we returned to bury Georgia.

We arrived from Indiana heartsick, but knowing we had to face Georgia's viewing and funeral. As we drove up our driveway our house seemed to glow. We gazed wonderingly at sparkling windows and neatly edged flowerbeds dotted with new plants. When we opened the front door and stepped into our immaculate home, the service of these sisters encircled us in tender comfort and welcome. The house was clean from top to bottom. The refrigerator was filled with food. There lingered in the very atmosphere a goodness and loveliness bestowed upon us by sisters who knew how to comfort those who stand in need of comfort.

Converted, covenant-keeping sisters carry with them the blessings of heaven and the glory of God. They receive the spiritual power and inspiration that comes when they keep their covenants. They turn their hearts to Jesus Christ and take His yoke upon themselves. And then, with healed and strengthened faith, converted sisters reach out to heal and strengthen others.

carry with you. The Savior is to be looked at as the Messiah, the Redeemer of the world. His teachings are auxiliary to that fact."[1]

More adamant in his warning, C. S. Lewis issued the same caution:

"I'm trying here to prevent anyone saying the really foolish thing that people often say about Him: 'I'm ready to accept Jesus as a great moral teacher, but I don't accept His claim to be God.' That is the one thing we must not say. A man who was merely a man and said the sort of things Jesus said would not be a great moral teacher. He would either be a lunatic—on a level with the man who says he's a poached egg—or else he would be the Devil of Hell. You must make your choice. Either this man was, and is, the Son of God: or else a madman or something worse. You can shut Him up for a fool, you can spit at Him and kill Him as a demon; or you can fall at His feet and call Him Lord and God. But let us not come with any patronising nonsense about His being a great human teacher. He has not left that open to us. He did not intend to."[2]

This is an important distinction to remember in any discussion about Jesus' teaching methodology.

METHODOLOGY #1: TEACH BY LIVING THE GOSPEL

We begin, therefore, by acknowledging that Jesus often taught His gospel best by the way He lived. He teaches by example. This principle becomes clearer when reading the New Testament book of Mark on its own. If you will study the Gospel of Jesus according to Mark, you'll notice the focus is on what Jesus *did* more than what He *said*. Particularly noticeable is that Mark didn't include any lengthy sermons of Jesus which are recorded in the other Gospels. Mark seems to be testifying that if you never heard Jesus preach but merely watched the way He treated others, responded to persecution, and reverenced God's law, you would likely conclude, "Truly this was the Son of God," as did the Roman centurion who watched Jesus die on the cross (Matthew 27:54). People were impressed to follow Him because of the way they felt when they were around Him.

Mark recorded an important observation about the Savior's humility and character: "And . . . rising up a great while before day, he went out, and departed into a solitary place, and there prayed" (Mark 1:35). Jesus didn't just talk about prayer. He didn't just model for His disciples how to pray. He prayed alone—when no one was watching. He prayed because He believed in the power of daily communication with His Father. Most likely early in the morning, "a great while before day," afforded the most likely time when He wasn't surrounded by a multitude and could engage in essential personal prayer.

Some of the scribes and Pharisees at the time of Jesus's ministry provide a contrast to the Savior's authentic approach to living the Gospel. Matthew reported Jesus saying, "All therefore whatsoever [the scribes and Pharisees] bid you observe, that observe and do; but do not ye after their works: for they say, and do not" (Matthew 23:3). These particular scribes and Pharisees could teach some fine gospel lessons; however, mixed messages occurred because they didn't live those teachings themselves. Their daily lives nullified the power of the word.

The Savior's example at the Last Supper gives us another snapshot of preaching a sermon by the way He treated others. In evidence of incredible humility, Jesus performed a duty that no Jew could be required to do, even Jewish servants. He washed the feet of each of the Twelve and then said, "For I have given you an example, that ye should do as I have done to you. Verily, verily, I say unto you, the servant is not greater than his lord; neither he that is sent greater than he that sent him" (John 13:15–16). Then He added, "If ye know these things, happy are ye if ye do them" (v. 17).

Living the gospel authentically makes us naturally joyful. Furthermore, that joy reflects in our countenances. It is real. It is meaningful. Such service is not a duty. To humble ourselves and fully accept that there is no assignment so lowly, no task that is too minor or that isn't visible or doesn't count enough, allows us to teach the joy of service and obedience the way the Savior taught.

I take another example of teaching by example from the Book of Mormon. The story of Ammon as a missionary to the Lamanites is a favorite for most of us. How do you open a foreign society for preaching the gospel that had so many biases against the Nephites when you're a Nephite missionary? One of the Lamanite kings, Lamoni, offered Ammon his daughter in marriage when Ammon was taken prisoner. Ammon's response to Lamoni is surprising when you think of what the king was offering. Ammon answered, "Nay, but I will be thy servant" (see Alma 17:20–25). It was in doing all that the king commanded of him, in demonstrating what it means to truly serve and love your enemies, that brought the Lamanites to notice the power that attended Ammon in his work. Soon afterwards, King Lamoni thinks that Ammon is the very one he is trying to emulate—Jesus Christ, or "the Great Spirit," as the Lamanites identified Him (see Alma 18:10–18). In this way, Ammon orchestrated an ideal learning environment in which to teach the truths of the gospel.

He prepared his "students" to believe the doctrine he explained because he first lived those truths as a daily approach to life.

I put the mothers of the 2,000 stripling warriors on this list of those who taught by example. We often underscore that they taught faith in such a way that their sons remained faithful in the middle of war. Furthermore, the manner in which these boys lived faith in turn taught and strengthened the prophet Helaman, who learned by watching their examples. This is truly remarkable. How did those mothers teach such faith? Their messages clearly reached those sons, who testified, "We do not doubt our mothers knew it" (Alma 56:48). At least some of these women, if not a large number of them, had lost their husbands when they laid down their lives rather than go to war again because of a covenant they made (see Alma 24). Day in and day out, these mothers made choices to keep that sacred covenant, regardless of the hardships that surely came their way. In April 2016 general conference, President Monson challenged us to "choose the harder right instead of the easier wrong."[3] Consider how often those mothers must have chosen the harder right—again and again. Their sons watched them as those women put God first and trusted in Him because His plan is the only true way to proceed. There must have been very difficult times. I don't see those mothers sitting down in an organized family home evening with a PowerPoint or a little bulletin board and pictures, saying, "Sons, tonight our lesson is about faith. Let me tell you what faith is and how to live by faith." I believe that those sons knew faith because they saw their mothers live by faith, making difficult choices that indicated their commitment to Christ, most likely over several years when the mothers weren't thinking those sons even noticed.

I remember an application paper assignment I gave a first-year

Book of Mormon class at Brigham Young University. For his paper, one of the boys in the class chose the story of the stripling warriors, then called his mother to tell her what a difference her example made to establish his faith. Being away from home for the first time, he had come to realize what she had done for him throughout his life—little things that mothers never recognize because such actions are just natural. Your faithful actions make a difference, and not only do your children see them, your sisters in Relief Society notice, your neighbors instinctively see, your husband recognizes the influence, and your grandchildren feel the strength of your choices. Faithful actions are powerful.

Saint Francis of Assisi, for whom Pope Francis took his name, is given credit for saying, "Preach the gospel always. Use words only when necessary."

METHODOLOGY #2: FOCUS ON PRINCIPLES RATHER THAN EXCEPTIONS

Now consider a second methodology that Jesus used to teach: focus on the principle and not the exception. As teachers and parents, our students and children often ask us, "Is it appropriate for me to do such-and-such. If yes, then when can I do it?" In our responses, it is tempting to focus on the exception without identifying the principle and the reasons why the principle is important.

I first recognized the power of emphasizing the principle rather than the exception when President Gordon B. Hinckley was first named as President of the Church in 1995. He held a press conference, which was unusual at the time, as I recall. I remember that the first or second reporter asked President Hinckley what he thought about women working outside the home, a topic discussed by President Ezra Taft Benson about eight years earlier.[4] Faithful women in the Church had interpreted his teachings in a variety of ways that often resulted in divisions and hurt feelings in many congregations. Now, before President Hinckley had even had a chance to address the Church in an official capacity, a reporter asked what I considered to be a no-win question: "President Hinckley, what do you think about women working outside the home?" I remember groaning as I watched the press conference on television, "Oh, what a dastardly thing to do. This is the end for President Hinckley." What could he answer that wouldn't sound like he was throwing President Benson under the bus . . . or else reinforce the misunderstandings of what President Benson taught?

I heard President Hinckley start talking about children. He talked about how wonderful they are and how quickly they grow up and how easily taught they are, how moldable they are. I became more uneasy as I listened because I thought he was dodging the reporter's question. After establishing the important principle of children in the Lord's plan, however, President Hinckley said something like, "You know, mothers are going to need to do the best they can in their circumstances." What a stunning teaching moment. He wisely avoided the bait by focusing on the eternal principle in the question. The issue is not whether or not women should work outside the home; there are innumerable and various reasons to be considered. The fundamental constant on this topic is the children. How are parents ensuring their children are protected, nurtured, and loved? If you read President Benson's talk to women today, looking for the principle rather than exceptions, you will note that he taught the same truth as did President Hinckley—remember your children's needs as you consider employment opportunities and financial decisions.

Here is an illustration from Jesus of this same approach to

teaching. The Pharisees asked Jesus, "Is it lawful for a man to put away his wife for every cause?" (Matthew 19:3). In other words—when am I justified to divorce my spouse? The Jewish law, as these leaders interpreted it, required that a man obtain only a letter of divorcement from a legal official. However, what did Jesus start talking about in his answer to them? This is fabulous. Does he talk about justifiable reasons for divorce? No, he focused on marriage and the sanctity of marriage: "Have ye not read, that he which made them at the beginning made them male and female, and said, For this cause shall a man leave father and mother, and shall cleave to his wife: and they twain shall be one flesh? . . . What therefore God hath joined together, let not man put asunder" (vv. 4–6). Jesus was reminding these leaders to focus on the principle and then do the best you can in those circumstances. We can spend too much time talking about exceptions rather than the principle, which confuses the real question. When the principle is clear, individuals are in a much better position to find the best personal application for their circumstances.

METHODOLOGY #3: RECOGNIZE VALUE IN EVERY PERSON

For my third methodology, Jesus focused on the value of each individual. Amid the multitudes that often surrounded Him, he saw individual sons and daughters of God. The Savior's encounter with the woman who touched the hem of His garment illustrates this principle well. When a mass of people clamored around Jesus as He passed by, this woman, whose name we do not know, reached out and touched the hem of his clothing, suggesting she was already laying or sitting on the ground (see Mark 5:25–34; see also Luke 8:43–48). She appears to have wanted no one to notice her. But Jesus noticed. He knew her and drew her out from the crowd.

Nicodemus, an important Jewish leader, came in the middle of the night to talk to Jesus (John 3:1–21). Did he not have time in his daily schedule to talk to Jesus? No. He didn't want anyone else to see him when he came, so he came in the middle of the night to learn from Jesus. In this unusual setting, Jesus taught one individual a remarkable lesson about being born again. He gave a man with shaky motivation His complete attention and best thinking. To Nicodemus in the middle of the night is the only time that scripture records Jesus's witness, "For God so loved the world, that he gave his Only Begotten Son" (John 3:16). Does Jesus love and care about Nicodemus? Did the fact that He responded to Nicodemus's visit with compassion despite the late hour make a difference? We read that Nicodemus later defended Jesus in front of all the Sanhedrin (John 7:45–52) and, after the Crucifixion, put his reputation on the line to assist Joseph of Arimathea in ensuring a respectful burial for Jesus (John 19:38–42).

In the next chapter of John, Jesus met a Samaritan woman at the well in middle of the day (John 4:6–7). By drawing water six hours after sunrise, I think she was trying to avoid anybody else, especially the other women who drew water much earlier in the day. How would other women in the village respond to her? She'd had five husbands and the man she was living with was not her husband (4:16–18). She would have been marginalized among her own people, as well as the Jews. But Jesus taught her about living water—when no one else was around.

Years ago, I taught the ten-year-olds in my ward Primary. There were eight ten-year-olds in the class; seven or eight of them attended every week. One week, however, only one of the eight came to our class. Taylor was the only one in town that weekend. When it was time to begin class, Taylor looked around and asked, "Where is everyone?" I responded, "Taylor, I guess it's just you and me." He asked, "So what are we going to do? Play hangman?" Before I answered, I remembered the example of Christ teaching Nicodemus alone and also the woman at the well when she was alone. I told him briefly about these stories. Then ten-year-old Taylor said begrudgingly, "I guess we need to have a lesson." He and I sat around the little table in the room and he took out his notebook I provided the children to record ideas from each lesson. I still remember that the lesson was on the baptism of Jesus Christ. Taylor showed me from his scriptures what he knew about the story and I taught him some other things that I knew. He marked some new things in his scriptures, and we did some pictures to illustrate some symbolism, and the next week all eight members of the class were back again. Taylor showed them his notebook and said, "This is what we did last week." And the kids said, "You didn't play hangman?" "No, we did this," and he showed it to them. Then they said to me, "Are we going to do the same lesson you did with Taylor last week?" and I said, "No, we get to do the next one now." That was in February. At the end of the year, I gave them their notebooks. One of them asked again, "What about the lesson that only Taylor got? Do we have it in here?" Now, nothing was extra special in that one lesson—except a wonderful opportunity to teach one individual with as much care as we would an auditorium filled with people. If we truly value each person as a beloved son or daughter of God, we will see individuals rather than a group whenever we teach.

METHODOLOGY #4: PROVIDE
TOOLS FOR SELF-DISCOVERY

People asked Jesus questions all the time. Some of them were sincere; others were asked with the hope of trapping Him to make a mistake. Often Jesus avoided providing an obvious answer, but rather encouraged the questioner to ask more questions that could lead him or her to discover a solution through critical thinking. He did not appear to be anxious to give them an answer instantaneously. Sometimes finding answers takes time. Something about that process of learning and connecting truths is even more instructive than learning an answer. Jesus created an environment where people learned more through the Spirit than He verbally taught and where He encouraged critical-thinking skills.

Here's an example. Jesus and His apostles were in Caesarea Philippi, where He promised Peter the keys of the kingdom (Matthew 16:19). But first the Savior asked the Twelve, "Whom do men say that I the Son of Man am?" (v. 13). From their answers, it appears that no one was announcing one clear explanation for His identity. People were saying all kinds of different things: John the Baptist returned to life or one of the Old Testament prophets like Jeremiah or Elijah (v. 14). The point is, Jesus did not go out and tell people who He was. Never do we read that during His mortal ministry, He commissioned the apostles to go out as missionaries to announce that the Son of God was living among them, that the Messiah was come and where they could find Him. What we do read is that Jesus commissioned the Twelve to "preach, saying, The kingdom of heaven is at hand" (Matthew 10:7).

When Jesus asked the Twelve, "But whom say *ye* that I am?" I think the tone of their "class" changed dramatically. Peter answered, "Thou art the Christ, the Son of the Living God." And how did Jesus respond? "Blessed art thou, Simon Bar-jona: for flesh and blood hath not revealed it unto thee" (Matthew 16:15–17). No mortal person taught Peter this truth. That includes Jesus, who was at that time "flesh and blood." How was this foundational truth revealed to Peter? By the "Father which is in heaven," as revealed through the Holy Spirit (v. 17). The only way anyone ever learns or has learned Jesus's true identity is by revelation from God through the Holy Ghost (see 1 Corinthians 12:3). It's the same today. Jesus knew that the Spirit teaches truth about Him better than by His word.

President Joseph Fielding Smith taught this powerful truth: "The Spirit of God speaking to the spirit of man has power to impart truth with greater effect and understanding than the truth can be imparted by personal contact even with heavenly beings. Through the Holy Ghost the truth is woven into the very fibre and sinews of the body so that it cannot be forgotten."[5] Did you get that? The best way to learn is Spirit to spirit—even greater than if a heavenly being were to stand in front of us and teach us. That is a powerful reminder to us. This is the same way we are taught in the temple, isn't it?

Consider the story of Jesus feeding the 5,000. Jesus wanted more from His disciples than for them to notice the multitude who were growing hungry out in the wilderness. He needed them to be more than compassionate guides who would remind them to return home soon so they could eat (see Matthew 14:15). If Jesus then told them, "Don't worry. I'll feed them," I can see the disciples gratefully responding with something like, "Oh, wonderful. Perhaps we could hand out the napkins for you." But that's not what Jesus said. He directed them, "Give ye them to eat" (v. 16). They must have felt panic—this was hardly the assignment they expected. Jesus wanted to teach them that He had truly given them power—His power, which would prove vital for their success after He was gone. Notice that it was while the Twelve distributed the five loaves and two small fishes that the grace of God came upon them. Suddenly they were able to accomplish a mission well beyond their natural ability (vv. 19–21; see also John 6:5–13).

That same night, the Twelve went in their boat out on the water and Jesus went into the wilderness. A storm kept the disciples battling the water most of the night. They were frightened. The last time they struggled to get to shore, Jesus was with them. They awoke him and He calmed the waters. They knew from this experience that Jesus had power over the elements (see Mark 4:37–41). This time, however, Jesus was not with them. He had created an environment in which they could reinforce the lesson He taught them when they fed the 5,000. Had they learned what He wanted them to understand about His power in them? They would have been dripping wet and cold. It was dark. They feared for their lives. Then, to make the situation worse, they looked up to see what appeared to be a ghost out on the water. They couldn't know that it was actually Jesus. Jesus knew they saw Him and were frightened. He immediately called out, "Be of good cheer; it is I; be not afraid" (Matthew 14:27). The Twelve faced a situation that stretched their faith to the edge. Even without the ability to see with his physical eyes, Peter experimented on the word. In a stunning show of faith, Peter cried out, "Lord, if it be thou, bid me come unto thee on the water" (v. 28). Peter didn't know for sure, but he was ready to walk into the darkness if prompted. Jesus answered with one word: "Come" (v. 29).

To anyone who says that Peter didn't have faith in that situation, I answer, "Are you kidding me? If Peter lacked faith, what do you say about the eleven that stayed back in the boat?" Peter climbed out of the boat and he walked on tumultuous water. When he fell—and he did fall when he focused on the waves instead of Jesus—Jesus reached out immediately to grab him, saying, "Thou of little faith, wherefore didst thou doubt?" (v. 31). I don't think Jesus was disappointed with Peter at all. I think He was thrilled. As much faith as Peter had at that moment, however, would not be sufficient faith for what lay ahead. What an incredible approach Jesus used to reinforce to Peter the lesson that He had given them His power to do whatever He commanded.

In a similar way, Jesus did not answer the Samaritan woman's questions in a simple, easy way. The answer became apparent through a process. She first saw him as just another Jewish man traveling by her village (see John 4:8–10). Jesus directed the conversation toward living water and the patriarch Jacob, which sparked curiosity in her and led her to refer to Him with respect (see vv. 11–12). His comments were leading her gradually to discover the great truth. She became more interested in Him, as shown by her request, in essence: Give me this water, this living water you just told me about so I don't have to come back to this well. Jesus continued to prod her thinking by requesting her to bring her husband to join them in this talk. The purpose of this line of thought was not to shame her for the misfortune of so many failed marriages or living with a man who was not her husband, but to help her recognize that He knew all about her. The woman was learning rapidly, as shown by her theory, "Sir, I perceive that thou art a prophet" (v. 19). This is significant in that Samaritans and Jews looked for the Messiah to be a prophet like Moses (see Deuteronomy 18:15, 18). Still leading the woman to connect the dots, Jesus explained that *location* is not essential for worship but *how* one worships God: "They that worship him must worship him in spirit and in truth" (John 4:24).

Notice that the first one to actually mention the Christ or the Messiah was the woman, not Jesus. She told Him what the Spirit had led her to conclude from their conversation: "I know that Messias cometh, which is called Christ: when he is come, he will tell us all things" (John 4:25). Jesus then confirmed the truth she witnessed when He said, "I am speaketh unto thee" (see v. 26; I changed the order of the words to clarify the statement; Jesus is the Great I Am).

The scripture narratives portray Jesus as a master teacher who relied on the Holy Ghost to "teach . . . all things" (John 14:26). He further demonstrated that, with the Spirit as our companion, we can be more effective teachers when we:

1. Live what we teach.
2. Focus on principles, not exceptions.
3. Value each individual as a daughter or son of God.
4. Provide tools for self-discovery by serving others, stretching our faith, and developing critical thinking skills.

May we invite the Spirit to always teach us. May we strive to follow the Savior's example. Then, as we teach, may that Spirit be present to take the message into the hearts, the fibers, and the very sinews of those we get to teach so that all will be edified. I bear witness that through a setting-apart blessing, every teacher in the Church is promised authority to draw on the powers of heaven to succeed.

THE TEST OF LIFE

Bonnie L. Oscarson

A short time ago, as I pulled up to stop at a red light while driving in my car, I glanced out of my window and saw something which, for some reason, caught my attention and really moved me. There was a young man sitting on the grass in front of a neighborhood business about twenty feet away—and he was in the depths of sorrow. He was seated with his arms around his knees and his head bowed down. His shoulders were shaking as he wept uncontrollably. Seated next to him was a young woman who was trying to comfort and console him; she stroked his arm and laid her hand on his back, but he hardly seemed to notice, he was so consumed in his grief.

As I was about to pull away, she finally stood behind him and, bending over him, she wrapped her arms completely around his shoulders and seemed to be trying to cover him in comfort. He continued to weep uncontrollably. As I watched, I felt a portion of his grief. I finally had to pull away and lose sight of this touching scene, but the thought that came to my mind was *Sometimes this life can be so hard, so painful, and so very sad.*

Immediately, I had another thought. Whatever grief that

unknown young man was feeling had already been felt by the Savior. His pains and his sorrows had already been experienced and were understood. In my mind, I multiplied this man's grief and pain to include *all* of the sorrow, *all* of the pain, and *all* of the hurt, that comes as a result of sin, evil, abuse, or from any of the inevitable problems coming from living in a fallen world, that have taken place since the world began. In that moment of contemplation, the weight of the total combined suffering of all mankind felt incomprehensible.

The Savior, Jesus Christ, *willingly volunteered* to experience and take upon Himself all of the pain, the sorrow, and the suffering that every individual who has ever lived upon this earth from beginning to end would experience. Agreeing to accept this seemingly impossible task and having the courage and determination to follow through to the very end must indisputably go down for all eternity as the ultimate act of sacrifice, valor, and obedience. While the Savior fulfilled His assignment willingly, we know that he did so with "exceeding" sorrow (Mark 14:34) and trembling "because of pain" (Doctrine and Covenants 19:18). The fate of all mankind rested on His shoulders and the task that lay before Him was crushing. His own words in the Garden of Gethsemane give us a hint of what He felt, "O my Father, if it be possible, let this cup pass from me: *nevertheless* not as I will, but as thou wilt" (Matthew 26:39; emphasis added). This scripture is at the heart of my message today. The example of the Savior, Jesus Christ, who sensed the crushing weight of what lay before Him, who was also willing to say the words, "nevertheless, not as I will, but as thou wilt." This then exemplifies the test of life for each of us. It is the test of our true discipleship. Are we willing to say to our Father, "nevertheless," and then give up what we may want for what our Heavenly Father would have for us?

The scriptural instructions are clear about what is expected of us. The Savior set the example when He said, "I am Jesus Christ; I came by the will of the Father, and I do his will" (Doctrine and Covenants 19:24). He also gives us a charge, "Not every one that saith unto me, Lord, Lord, shall enter into the kingdom of heaven; but he that doeth the will of my Father who is in heaven" (3 Nephi 14:21). The Savior invites each of us to follow His example and do those things which our Father in Heaven would have us do.

WHAT THIS LOOKS LIKE IN DAY-TO-DAY LIVING

I'm afraid that I too often embody what is implied in the scripture "the spirit indeed is willing, but the flesh is weak" (Matthew 26:41) when it comes to putting the will of the Father before my own. I have made the decision to be a covenant-keeping disciple of Christ and I'm not guilty of committing what Elder Neal A. Maxwell called the "telestial sins"[1] but at times I still tend to withhold a small portion from the Lord because I have a few "favorite sins" or because I would rather spend my time on worldly or frivolous pursuits than on asking what the Lord would have me do.

Remember the cautionary tale described in Acts 5 about Ananias and his wife, Sapphira? It was at a time when the Saints had all things in common. Ananias and Sapphira sold a piece of land and then withheld a portion of the profit from the sale for themselves, rather than giving it all to the Apostles as was expected. I have always been somewhat surprised by the dire consequences they each suffered for their dishonesty. They were each struck dead as their duplicity was revealed (see Acts 5:1–11).

Perhaps one of the points of this story (besides the obvious lesson of integrity) is instruction on how seriously the Lord takes our willingness to lay *everything* on the altar for Him. I find it instructive to occasionally ask myself, "What am I holding back?"

We all have our justifications for our sometimes less-than-noble choices. Here's my rather dazzling justification: I work hard at my calling, I spend a lot of time fulfilling my responsibilities, don't I deserve to indulge myself sometimes? Elder Maxwell once observed, "Many of us thus have sufficient faith to avoid the major sins of commission, but not enough faith to sacrifice our distracting obsessions or to focus on our omissions."[2]

Please don't misunderstand what I am suggesting here. I think that all of us need to take time for ourselves—to recharge our batteries, so to speak. Women, and especially mothers who are deep in the trenches of taking care of the many needs around them—their children, their parents, their callings, their careers, their homes—need a break from the daily treadmill of routine to help maintain balance and keep joy in the journey. But I think we have all felt the promptings from the Spirit which nag at the edges of our conscience telling us that we could make better use of our "down time." I know I have.

In a world where our existence is not dependent on us milking the cows, feeding the chickens, growing our own food, or making the clothes we wear, it is easy to get caught up in the "thick of thin things"[3] and spend an inordinate amount of time on things that the prophet Moroni describes as "[having] no life," while we let "the hungry, and the needy, and the naked, and the sick and the afflicted to pass [us] by, and [we] notice them not" (Mormon 8:39). We often become more obsessed with getting to the gym every day or spending time reading and sending messages and photos on social media than we do visiting a neighbor face-to-face or making the effort to actually call a friend to see how they are doing or even just read the lesson to prepare for next Sunday's class. Surely we are capable of finding the right balance in our lives as we seek the influence of the Spirit to give us direction.

Elder Maxwell makes the point like this: "So many of us are kept from eventual consecration because we mistakenly think that, somehow, by letting our will be swallowed up in the will of God, we lose our individuality (see Mosiah 15:7). What we are really worried about, of course, is not giving up self, but selfish things—like our roles, our time, our preeminence, and our possessions. No wonder we are instructed by the Savior to lose ourselves (see Luke 9:24). He is only asking us to lose the old self in order to find the new self. It is not a question of one's losing identity but of finding his true identity! Ironically, so many people already lose themselves anyway in their consuming hobbies and preoccupations but with far, far lesser things."[4]

I believe that earnestly seeking to know what the Lord would have us spend our time doing, with the sincere intention of following what He directs us to do, will result in some wonderfully elevating course corrections in our lives.

There is a story which appeared in the *Friend* magazine a few years ago in which Elder Gerald N. Lund shared the following story from his own life. As a young man he had always planned to serve a mission until the time came to actually do it. He had a serious girlfriend, had just started a good job, was making good money, and he had just bought a new car. All of a sudden being away for two whole years didn't sound very attractive! He decided that he would stay at home and serve as a stake missionary instead. His wise father took the news fairly well but said to him, "'Well, that's your choice. But it's a pretty big decision. Would you be willing to take two separate days to go off by yourself somewhere and fast and pray about this? If you do and you still feel the same way, I will not say another word.'"

Young Gerald agreed immediately because he felt certain that the Lord was supportive of his decision not to serve a full-time mission. He took his scriptures up into the mountains one Saturday and fasted, read, and prayed. He went home and told his dad, "'My feelings haven't changed.'" His father smiled and said, "'You promised me two days.'"

The next week found him again up in the mountains on a Sunday morning where he again studied and prayed until it was time to go to Church in the afternoon. He still felt the same way about not serving a mission and he wanted to hurry down and tell his father. He picked up his girlfriend and they went to sacrament meeting.

Here is how he describes what happened next, "During the meeting I idly picked up the hymnbook. It fell open to the hymn that in those days was called 'It May Not Be on the Mountain Height.' Part of me said, 'Don't read it!' But I read all three verses, including the words 'I'll go where you want me to go, dear Lord.' In that instant my heart and mind changed. When I finished reading, I closed the book and looked up. Tears were streaming down my girlfriend's face. She said, 'You're going, aren't you?' I said, 'Yes, I am.'" He concludes the story with, "I can't imagine where my life would have gone if I had chosen to stay home. My mission led me to great happiness."[5]

Elder Lund's final comment points out the paradoxical thing about putting the Lord's will above our own. You would think that giving up what we want to do for what the Lord wants us to do would cause us to feel somewhat deprived, secretly resentful, or would produce a martyr mentality. In the Lord's loving generosity, just the opposite is true. When we allow our personal desires to be swallowed up in the will of the Lord, a marvelous change begins to take place in our souls and the blessings begin to pour in.

An Apostle of the Lord has promised, "Only by aligning our wills with God's is full happiness to be found. Anything less results in a lesser portion."[6] Do we want a full measure of happiness in this life? Then we need to be willing to give a full measure of obedience and service.

Elder Maxwell says that as we learn to submit our will to the Lord we will receive "an enhanced capacity for joy." He quotes Brigham Young who said, "'If you want to *enjoy exquisitely,* become a Latter-day Saint, and then live the doctrine of Jesus Christ.'"[7]

SERVICE

In my experience, if we want to do the will of the Father, we need to find ways to serve those around us. Isn't that the Savior's message again and again in the scriptures? Service does several things: it invites the Spirit into our lives, and it helps us forget our own worries and makes us happy. As we take care of those around us, it also helps us accomplish Heavenly Father's work.

I believe there is one prayer that will always be answered and that is, "Lord, show me who I can serve today." I recently heard a quote from President James E. Faust which has stuck in my mind because it is so needed in today's self-centered, self-serving world. He said, "The problem is that too many of us try to *consume* happiness rather than *generate* it."[8]

Instead of taking the attitude of "What am I going to get out of this?" as we go about our daily lives and, specifically, as we attend Church meetings and classes, what if we were to ask instead, "Who can I lift and serve?" What difference would it make in the lives of our children and youth if we taught them that they don't just attend church on Sunday and activities during the week because of what *they* will get out of it, but also because of what they have to *offer*—because there might be someone there who needs their friendship and encouragement. I think both we and our youth need to know that part of living the gospel and doing the will of our Heavenly Father is to watch out for His other children. Do we realize how much we are needed to do that each week? Do we teach our children that they are an important part of the work that goes on in a ward family and that what they have to offer others can be not just truly valuable but essential?

OTHER BLESSINGS

Elder David A. Bednar has described other blessings we receive when we show our willingness to align our will with the Lord's: "We come to know the Savior as we do our best to go where He wants us to go, as we strive to say what He wants us to say, and as we become what He wants us to become. As we submissively acknowledge our total dependence upon Him, He enlarges our capacity to serve ever more effectively. Gradually, our desires align more completely with His desires, and His purposes become our purposes."[9]

Don't you love those blessings? As we learn to heed the prompting of the Spirit as to what the Lord would have us do each day, we become more like the Savior and our capacity to serve more effectively continues to increase. If we continue on the path of aligning our will to the Lord's, we gradually become one in purpose with our Heavenly Father and His Son.

As our purposes align, we receive another great blessing to help us in this life. Elder Maxwell said, "As one's will is increasingly submissive to the will of God, he can receive inspiration and revelation so much needed to help meet the trials of life."[10]

SUBMITTING TO THE LORD'S WILL IN THE MIDST OF TRIALS

There are many whose trials with submission do not come because of misguided priorities or choices they have personally made. Many suffer the consequences of decisions others have made, such as infidelity, abuse, and addictions. There are also trials that happen simply because this life is meant to be a period of testing. Illness, whether mental or physical, accidents, natural disasters, and the death of loved ones are trials which all of us will deal with at one point or another. For some, despite all they have done to prepare, their lives don't turn out as they would have chosen. There are many who desire marriage but for whom the right opportunity has not presented itself, and there are others who desperately want to be mothers but struggle with infertility. It is hard at times to trust that these kinds of challenges are also a part of God's plan for His children. Speaking of one of the purposes of this earth life, the Lord has declared, "And we will prove them herewith, to see if they will do all things whatsoever the Lord their God shall command them" (Abraham 3:25).

The challenges and trials of life, even those we do not bring upon ourselves through our agency, are also a test of our willingness to submit to the Lord in that we must decide how we will react to them. Some people allow trials to challenge their faith in God's purposes because they question whether or not a just God would allow such things to happen. Others question whether or not God exists at all when trials seem randomly heaped upon them.

How should a covenant-keeping daughter of God view the trials that come to her through no fault of her own? If she can keep an eternal perspective, even in trying times, she will begin to see challenges as opportunities for growth as she trusts in the Lord to help. President Russell M. Nelson recently taught us, "God so loved the world that He sent His Only Begotten Son to help us. And His Son, Jesus Christ, gave His life for us. All so that we could have access to godly power—power sufficient to deal with the burdens, obstacles, and temptations of our day."[11]

If we are truly "converted unto the Lord" (Alma 23:8), we will not let our trials and challenges shake our faith that we *are* daughters of a loving Heavenly Father, that He *does* love us and wants to bless us, and that trials are not an indication that God has forsaken us. Rather, we will continue to seek to understand what we are to learn from adversity, remain steadfast and worthy, and continue to serve those around us.

I cannot help but believe that there is a tender place in the heart of our Heavenly Father for His daughters and sons who suffer because of the choices of others. He wants us to stay close to Him, to turn to Him, and to let Him help us carry our burdens. I testify He will be there to help us through our challenges.

WHAT ELSE MATTERS?

I want to conclude with a story told by President Gordon B. Hinckley that to me sums up so well what is behind the need to submit our will to the will of the Lord. He told of meeting a man who was a naval officer from another country and who came to the United States for advanced training. He was not a Christian but he noticed the good behavior of some of his associates in his training and he asked them about their beliefs. They shared with him the story of the Savior's life and mission. They told him of the appearance of God the Father and His Son, Jesus Christ, to a young farm boy named Joseph Smith. They taught him of modern prophets. They taught him the gospel and as the Spirit touched his heart, he was baptized into the Church.

He met President Hinckley just before he was to return to his native land and President Hinckley recounts this about their meeting:

"I said, 'Your people are not Christians. . . . What will happen when you return home a Christian and, more particularly, a Mormon Christian?'

"His face clouded, and he replied, 'My family will be disappointed. I suppose they will cast me out. They will regard me as dead. As for my future and my career, I assume that all opportunity will be foreclosed against me.'

"I asked, 'Are you willing to pay so great a price for the gospel?'

"His dark eyes, moistened by tears, shone from his handsome brown face as he answered, 'It's true, isn't it?'

"Ashamed at having asked the question, I responded, 'Yes, it's true.'

"To which he replied, 'Then what else matters?'"[12]

I ask you the same question: If the gospel is true, what else matters? Sisters, I testify to you that the Church to which we belong, The Church of Jesus Christ of Latter-day Saints, is God's true Church on the earth. The authority to act with God's power and authority has been restored to the earth in these latter days through a prophet of God. I testify that Joseph Smith saw the Father and the Son in that sacred grove of trees and that he stands at the head of this dispensation as the revealer of Christ for our day. I testify that we have a living prophet who stands at the head of our Church today, who holds all the keys and powers to administer the Lord's work on the earth, and who receives guidance and revelation to accomplish that work. So what else matters?

I testify that Jesus Christ set the supreme example of submitting our will to the will of the Father. He willingly offered Himself to experience the pain, sorrows, and suffering of all mankind in order to redeem our souls from the sins and trials of this earth life. He accomplished the Atonement completely and totally—He went the full distance in "finish[ing His] preparations" (Doctrine and Covenants 19:19) for all mankind and showed us what it means to do the will of the Father.

I testify there are great blessings in store when we are also willing to say to the Father, "nevertheless, thy will be done" (see Doctrine and Covenants 109:44) and align our will to the will of the Lord. *This is the test of life.* As we become better at doing it we will find greater happiness, increased ability to receive personal revelation, greater capacity to serve those around us, more help in meeting trials, and a more Christlike character.

I am grateful for the opportunity to study and learn more about this subject. It has given me a greater determination to seek to understand what the Lord would have me do to serve Him. I pray that you have also received some insight or inspiration about what you can be doing to do His will.

THE GRANDEUR OF GOD

Matthew O. Richardson

When I first learned of my assigned topic, *The Grandeur of God,* my mind immediately thought of a well-worn book on our bookshelf. One of the great joys in my life has been reading stories to my children and grandchildren. Over the years, my wife and I have collected scores of books, and there is hardly anything better than settling in on a cozy sofa with a child nestled close enough they can take in both your voice and the pictures of a good story. Over the years, I have discovered that whenever I choose a book to read, it rarely aligns with the choice of those being read to. So my children or grandchildren do the selecting and I do the reading—complete with voices!

Somewhere along the line, our children kept bringing me the same book to read over and over. It eventually became the book that "only Dad can read!" Now all these years later, my grandchildren cozy up with the very same book and listen to their "Dadpa" read Fred Marcellino's award-winning rendition of *The Story of Little Babaji.*[1] You may know it. It is a story about a young boy named Babaji, who is the son of Mamaji and Papaji. One day, Babaji takes a walk in the jungle and "by and by" meets a tiger, who says, "Little Babaji, I'm going to eat you up!" Babaji begs for mercy and offers the Tiger his "beautiful little red coat." The Tiger takes Babaji's coat and proudly declares, "Now I'm the grandest tiger in the jungle" as he struts off. Little Babaji continues his jungle walk and has three separate encounters with other tigers along the way, who end up taking his trousers, shoes, and umbrella. Wearing a piece of Babaji's clothing, each tiger declares "Now I'm the grandest tiger in the jungle" before disappearing in the bush.

Now, you may be thinking, why in the world would Brother Richardson think of *Little Babaji* when considering the *Grandeur of God?* Where did that come from? Most likely it is because the word *grandeur* is from French, meaning "grand." And after reading the line, "Now I'm the grandest tiger in the jungle," hundreds of times, who *wouldn't* think of Little Babaji? Actually, there is more to it than that. I am intrigued by four tigers that were so distracted by the grandeur of Little Babaji's clothing that they would pass up a tasty meal. Even more intriguing is their conclusion that *possessing* something grand would actually make them grand. And then at the heart of it all is their insatiable desire to be the "grandest"—not just grand, but "the grandest tiger in all of the jungle."

As the story goes, all four tigers eventually meet up in the jungle and begin fighting, arguing about which of them is grandest. The fight escalates to the point where they discard Little Babaji's clothing and begin to tear at each other with their claws and teeth. They end up catching hold of each other's tails and circling a tree, "trying to eat each other up." They run and run until they melt away into a pool of butter. Yikes!

I worry that there is a little tiger in us all. Like the tigers and

Little Babaji's clothing, there is always something so grand that it is easy to get distracted, then enthused, possibly obsessed, and eventually immersed in it all. It is almost hypnotic. For example, I remember seeing a large crowd gathered in front of a store window when I was a boy. I worked my way to the glass and saw something so grand, I couldn't take my eyes off it. There in the store window was a television set playing a demo of the first home video game, called *Pong*. I, like everyone else, was mesmerized. My mind could hardly process this advanced gizmo of electronic wonder. Forget that it was only three years earlier that NASA had put a man on the moon and people had been blown away by that grandeur. But that was "so 1969," and now *Pong* was the grandest thing in the jungle. Like the tigers, I knew deep down, that if my family had *Pong*, we would be the grandest in the neighborhood. It couldn't possibly get any better.

Until 1977, that is. People could hardly digest the sensation of a full-sized battle cruiser rumbling overhead just after the opening credits of *Star Wars*, or then the much-larger Star Destroyer that's chasing it. It was a mind-blowing sensory rush of epic proportions. My teenage mind couldn't take in just how monstrous the ships were. How real they were. It was hard to believe that such euphoria was created by a model that was only 109 inches long but filmed in such a way this it appeared real.[2] For those who witnessed it for the first time at that time know that it was definitely the grandest thing in the jungle.

Until three years later. Sleek telephones, the Trimline models, made their way into the majority of US households. It wasn't so much the cool slim design, but the *buttons* that revolutionized the industry. It was magnificent; only those who had been using rotary-dial telephones could really understand the marvel of "push buttons"! Now that was the *grandest* thing in the jungle!

Until . . . cell phones became the staple of the day in 1984. Only James Bond had such gadgets. Impressive! But then in 1993, we saw the first "smartphone" that had a keypad for a pager, email, and even a stylus for writing (what's a stylus?). Could it be any more wondrous? Yep! In 2002, a camera was added, and in 2003 you could now text and browse the web. The pinnacle of miracles! Until 2007, when the iPhone was introduced, with a music player and a touchscreen. A jaw-dropping 1.4 million tigers had to have one. Then in 2009, a technology that was until then only available to the military, known as the Global Positioning System (GPS), was added into the mix. Awesome! This was a favorite feature for men, who could now get directions without having to ask another human. The great irony, however, was they still had to ask a woman! "Siri, how do I get home?" Soon your phone will slice, dice, make julienne fries, and even babysit . . . wait, it already does that! But keep in mind that it—true to the form of the past—will require yet another upgrade. What? You don't have the latest upgrade? Obviously, *you* must not be very grand!

Every few months, a new tiger takes the throne of its predecessor, who is tossed on a scrap heap of 8-track tapes, cassette tapes, chia pets, pet rocks, neopets, Rubik's cubes, bell bottoms, shoulder pads, bangs, *High School Musicals*, speed dating, leg warmers, and who knows how many other things. Our fascination and insatiable appetite for the "*grandest* thing in the jungle" seems to have become part of us. It reminds me of Paul describing the last days to Timothy. He said there will be those who have "itching ears" (2 Timothy 4:3). Sadly, it sounds as if those in the last days have an insatiable itch, but one that cannot be scratched.

When will enough be enough? When will something ever be truly awesome? By that I mean *lastingly* awesome? Something that doesn't need an upgrade?

Perhaps the problem is not so much the search for awesome, but our inability to identify, understand, and *believe* just what *awesome* really is. Only then can we find the cure for the itch, experience the peace of contentment, and the joy of lasting enlightenment. Only then can we be truly inspired. A current slang dictionary defines *awesome* as "something Americans use to describe everything." This only fuels the fire; the common dictionary definition doesn't provide much help either. There we find *awesome* synonymous with words like amazing, astonishing, astounding, marvelous, awful, eye-opening, fabulous, miraculous, portentous, prodigious, staggering, stunning, stupendous, sublime, surprising, wonderful, and wondrous.[3] Whew! All of these were once used in describing wonders like *Pong*, *Star Wars*, cell phones, and the rest of the heap already mentioned. It seems that awesome is only momentary. It lasts until we get bored with it, or the next *wow!* comes along. As a result, we are left yearning, searching, and longing for something . . . else. I believe that deep within us we long for something that extends beyond our own power or the power of others—beyond our reach. We yearn to feel or know that there is more to this life than possessing the grand of the moment. So rather than going to the dictionary to understand *grandeur* or *awesome*, we need to dig deeper.

The original meaning of *awesome* is simply "filled with awe." And *awe,* as you know, is defined as "a feeling of reverential respect mixed with fear or wonder." Rabbi Harold Kushner once described this state as "being in the presence of a power so overwhelming that it defines who you are."[4] He continues, "You may feel small, but you don't feel diminished. It's not fear. When you are afraid, you are overawed by something and you want to run away. When you feel reverent, you are overawed but you want to come closer."[5] While I have been in awe with technologies, social positions or status, or "things of the world," they never really defined me—at least not for long. But what else is there?

In the summer of 1830, twenty-six-year-old Emma Smith was wrestling with disappointment and deep worry. She received this counsel, "And verily I say unto thee that thou shalt lay aside the things of this world, and seek for the things of a better" (Doctrine and Covenants 25:10). Things of a better? Like what, for example? Before we can find the answer to that question, it appears that we must first "lay aside the things of the world." Perhaps this is easier said than done. Try fasting from your makeup, soda, Netflix, social media, or your phone. Take your phone, for example. Cal Newport, author of *Deep Work,* reports that smartphones and other devices cause the brain to be constantly distracted as there is a constant urge to check messages, updates to social media, notifications, and on and on. According to Newport, this distracts us from what is most important in our lives.[6]

What could possibly be more important than the things of the world? If we lay aside *those things*, then what is left to inspire us, fill us, motivate us, and enlighten us? Is there anything that awesome? President Gordon B. Hinckley said, "This is the Almighty of whom I stand in awe and reverence. It is He to whom I look in fear and trembling. It is He whom I worship and unto whom I give honor and praise and glory."[7] Am I suggesting that God is the thing of a better? Absolutely and without hesitation or equivocation. I cannot think of anything that rivals God. I cannot think of one thing that is *better* than God. Mormon explained, "Wherefore, all things which are good cometh of God" and "that which is of God inviteth and enticeth to do good continually; wherefore, every thing which inviteth and enticeth to do good, and to love God, and to serve him, is inspired of God" (Moroni 7:12, 13). Just how good is God? Can He be available? Omnipresent! Does He have power? Omnipotent! Does He have knowledge? Omniscient! Can he help? Omnicompassionate! I'll confess, I made that word up. But technically, it works! So does Omni*awesome* and Omni*grand!* God is the grandest of all. But, some may ask, how can you *know* that?

To answer this question, we must consider *knowing* in a different context than we may customarily use. The psalmist wrote, "Be still, and know that I am God" (Psalm 46:10). The word *know* in this scripture and throughout the Old Testament is from the Hebrew *yada'*. The easy translation of *yada'* is "to know." But Thomas Gromme explained that there is much more to it than that. He said, "For the Hebrews, *yada'* is more by the heart than by the mind, and the knowing arises not by standing back from in order to look at, but by active and intentional engagement in lived experience."[8] It is important to learn *about* God and his grandeur. It is critical, however, to *know* Him—through active and intentional engagement and by lived experience. So be still—or, in other words, lay aside the gizmos, gadgets, pride, fear, anger, doubt, habits, attitudes, and all things of the world—and *know* that God is grand.

"Oh, I tried that once," some may say, "but it didn't work out." May I strongly urge you to try again? We hear more regularly about people having a "crisis of faith." Most consider *crisis* to mean or describe "intense difficulty, trouble, or danger." Some attach synonyms such as "disaster, catastrophe, or calamity." I am confident that we have all experienced this concept of crisis—to some degree—in our lives, whether dealing with lack of faith, sickness, infidelity, immorality, uncertainty, heartbreak, mental or emotional, sickness, loss, pain, loneliness, disappointment, unfulfilled expectations, infertility, abuse, wayward family members, being single, divorced, unhappily married, or countless other circumstances. If you are experiencing a *crisis* in your life, will you please keep in mind that the word *crisis* is derived from Greek and actually means "decide" or "decision." Thus, a crisis of faith is not an insurmountable moment of disaster, but a moment to decide, a time to make a decision about your faith. At such a moment as this, I implore you to decide to give God a chance. Employ His grandeur. Isaiah boldly declared God's grandeur. According to Isaiah, all nations are a drop in the bucket compared to God. His power exalts every valley, lowers every mountain, makes straight the crooked, and smoothes every plain. While everything else fades, Isaiah reminds us that "God shall stand for ever" (Isaiah 40:8). God will feed his flock, gather His lambs, and carry them in his bosom. He will lead, counsel, and show the way to understanding. Isaiah then concludes, "Lift up your eyes on high, and behold who hath created these things, that bringeth out their host by number: he calleth them all by names by the greatness of his might, for that he is strong in power; not one faileth" (v. 26). And don't forget, Isaiah says, "He giveth power to the faint; and to them that have no might he increaseth strength" (v. 29). Ever the realist, Isaiah then warns, "Even the youths shall faint and be weary, and the young men shall utterly fall" (v. 30). Now, don't get discouraged, for Isaiah, in this wonderful sermon of God's grandeur, concludes by telling those in crisis—whatever that crisis may be, "But they that wait upon the Lord shall renew their strength; they shall mount up with wings as eagles; they shall run, and not be weary; and they shall walk, and not faint" (v. 31).

Please decide to intentionally draw nearer to God—especially in challenging times—rather than retreat from Him. Please decide that you won't abandon Him, even when it feels like He may have abandoned you. Brigham Young was once asked by a clerk in his office, "President Young, why is it that the Lord is not always at our side promoting universal happiness and seeing to it that the needs of people are met, caring especially for His Saints? Why is it so difficult at times?" Brigham responded, "It is the way it is because we must learn to be righteous in the dark."[9] So when it feels the darkest, when you can't find the answers, cannot see any possible means of deliverance, or feel so alone, will you please decide to trust in Him just a little longer? Finally, I plead with you that rather than turning to *Pong*, *Star Wars*, the internet, or any of the wonderful technologies past, present, or future, that you will lay aside the things of the world long enough to choose the grandest of them all.

God will make a difference, but will you? Can you? Do you? I *know* you can make a difference, because I have *personally* experienced in my heart and through intentional engagement the impact of women who understand the grandeur of God. C. S. Lewis wrote, "I believe in Christianity as I believe that the Sun has risen, not only because I see it, but because by it I see everything else."[10] I have known women in my life who have had a similar effect on me. They have allowed me to know (to experience) the grandeur of God *because of* the way they live their lives ever connected to God. A mother hauling children to church, planting seeds of faith, teaching us to pray, all while waiting for a husband to embrace the gospel. A diligent and enduring sister, dedicated mother-in-law, a believing and supportive grandmother-in-law, and so many other family members. And I cannot forget faith-filled Primary teachers, caring schoolteachers, and enthusiastic youth leaders. Surely they are the all the grandest in my jungle. Until . . . I met a young woman who not only understood the grandeur of God, but embraced it in every way. As such, God's grandeur became her grandeur. It is evident in her manner, her faith, her persistence, her obedience, and the way she treats others, especially me. In a very special way, she is the grandest in my heart's jungle.

I invite you to embrace God and all of His grandeur and by doing so, you will enact the scriptural promise that "he that receiveth my Father receiveth my Father's kingdom; therefore all that my Father hath shall be given unto him" (Doctrine and Covenants 84:38). By doing this, you—yes you—will be able to say with surety, "Now *I'm* among the grandest women in all the jungle."

STAY ON THE BUS: EXPERIENCING THE POWER OF JESUS CHRIST DEEPLY AND REGULARLY

Brad Wilcox

President Russell M. Nelson has encouraged members of the Church to access the power of Jesus Christ.[1] We have a word for that power. The word is *grace*. Grace is the power of Jesus Christ. Sister Sheri Dew, former member of the Relief Society general presidency, has defined grace as "the breathtaking scope of the Atonement of His Son and the power the Atonement makes available to us."[2] So as we strive to stay "converted unto the Lord" (3 Nephi 28:23), how do we experience the Lord's grace deeply and regularly? How do we accept President Nelson's challenge to draw the power of Jesus Christ into our lives?

I was with some Primary children teaching them about grace and I said, "Everyone grab a hymn book and we are going to play a little game. When I give you the signal I want you to start searching and let's see who can find the word *grace* the fastest. On your mark, get set, go!" The race was on and almost immediately a boy shouted out, "I found it!"

I said, "Wonderful! Which hymn?"

He responded, "'Called to Serve.'"

I quickly started reviewing the words in my mind because I

could not remember grace being in there. Finally, I asked, "Are you sure?"

"Yes!" the boy said and he held up the hymn book and pointed to the bottom of the page where we all discovered the hymn was written by Sister Grace Gordon. One of the teachers quipped, "Well, that puts a new twist on being saved by grace!" I could picture the children expecting Grace Gordon to show up in a superhero costume and save the day. Those children would not be the only ones to misunderstand what it means to be saved by grace. Many Christians believe that grace is just about getting us into heaven. Latter-day Saints know it also about becoming heavenly.

President Dieter F. Uchtdorf defined grace as "the divine assistance and endowment of strength by which we grow from the flawed and limited beings we are now into exalted beings."[3] In Hebrew, the word that was later translated as *grace* means "good will" or "favor given with compassion." Maybe that is why Christians through the centuries have used that word when describing God's good will, favor, and compassion. But grace is much more than a description of God's attributes. Grace is how God engages with us in developing those attributes. Grace is the strength He gives us to make us strong. It is the divine assistance He gives to make us divine.

Kenneth Cope is a beloved LDS singer and songwriter. He and I were together once speaking at a youth conference in Olympia, Washington. The theme was "The Time Is Now," and leaders had decorated the building with clocks on the tables, clock faces on the walls, and even an elaborate cardboard clock tower in the cultural hall. As the youth gathered in the chapel at the close of the conference for testimony meeting, they found a large glass-covered clock on an easel toward the front. The meeting proceeded in reverence until suddenly the easel broke and the clock came crashing to the floor. Glass shattered everywhere. The boy bearing his testimony at the time handled the situation ably. He said, "Well, I guess the time is no longer now. I guess the time is past!" Everyone laughed and several leaders hurried forward and began to clean up the mess so the meeting could continue. This same young man finished his testimony and said, "I'm sorry the clock broke. It can no longer remind us of the theme, but it can remind us that God loves broken things."

He was alluding to a song Kenneth wrote and had performed at the conference—a beautiful song that assures us that even when we waste the time God has given and we end up feeling like that clock, God still loves us and can help pick up the pieces and move us forward.[4]

One of the traditions I love about Brigham Young University Women's Conference is the instant choir. Each year any participant who would like is invited to join the choir. Then, with very limited practice, the group performs. This year our instant choir sang, "I stand all amazed at the love Jesus offers me, / Confused at the grace that so fully he proffers me."[5] When Charles H. Gabriel wrote that hymn, the word *confused* did not just mean "perplexed" or "disoriented." It also meant *overwhelmed*— standing in awe. Indeed, we should feel overwhelmed and in awe of the grace Jesus proffers us. *Proffers* is another word we don't use much anymore. It is more than a synonym for "offers." Adding the prefix *pro-* to *offers* indicates that instead of simply extending a gift to someone, the giver takes initiative to proactively place the gift before the receiver. The giver makes it almost impossible to refuse the gift because he or she places the gift right in the receiver's hands.

Think of the emblems of the sacrament. In many churches they are offered to the congregation and people must come forward to accept them. Not in our church. Latter-day Saints do not approach the front of the chapel to take them. Rather, the bread and water are proffered to us. They are literally placed before each of us individually—even when we are late and standing in the foyer (and don't ask me how I know that). This teaches us much about how lovingly the gift of grace is given.

Nevertheless, in Doctrine and Covenants 88:33 we read, "For what doth it profit a man if a gift is bestowed upon him, and he receive not the gift? Behold, he rejoices not in that which is given unto him, neither rejoices in him who is the giver of the gift." We have to be the ones who pick up the emblems. We have to be the ones who internalize them. We have to choose to engage with Christ who enables us to progress through this process we call redemption.

We stand all amazed at the grace Jesus proffers us, but He must stand a little amazed Himself at how many are unwilling to receive His generous gift—a gift that can save and transform us.

Receiving grace is like receiving a scholarship. It does not guarantee learning; it facilitates it. The donor of the scholarship does not want to get his or her money back. That is not the point. The donor wants to see the scholarship used. The gift is how the donor is helping the recipient learn, grow, progress, change, and become better. The scholarship recipient is not educated by the scholarship. Rather, the scholarship clears away obstacles and enables the recipient to become educated. It is the same with grace. The gift is not the end. It is a means to the desired end. As we show faith, repent, make and keep covenants, welcome the gift of the Holy Ghost, and endure to the end, we engage with Christ in the process of becoming more like Him.

The problem is that we want to reach that end immediately. We desire to be changed instantaneously. We want to be "poofed," Harry Potter style: Poof! You're spiritual! Poof! You're patient! Poof! You're charitable! We all want God to wave a magic wand so that the process of change is not so difficult. However, change without challenge is not change. Strength too easily won is not strength.

One young man wrote me from the MTC: "Where's God? When I need Him the most, why has He abandoned me?"

I responded, "What are you talking about? God *lives* at the MTC. He just visits everywhere else!"

In his next email the young elder wrote, "I have been here for three weeks and I still don't speak Spanish."

I reminded him how long it took him to learn English when he was a baby and told him he would need to be equally patient as he learns Spanish.

"But don't we believe in the gift of tongues?" he asked. He was looking for the magic wand: Poof! You speak Spanish!

I replied, "Of course we believe in the gift of tongues, and sometimes in Church history that has been instantaneous, but more often it has taken time." That fact is not because Christ's grace is not present, but because the purpose of the miracle is different. God doesn't just want this young missionary to act like he knows Spanish. He doesn't want him to learn enough phrases that he can fake it for a day or two. God wants him to teach the gospel and answer people's most heartfelt questions in Spanish. That means the language has to become part of him. Most important, God wants that kid to know how hard it is to change so that he can actually have a little empathy when he challenges someone to quit smoking, drinking, and living a promiscuous lifestyle. God wants the elder to understand that learning is a process and that failures, mistakes, and missteps are part of that process. God wants that knowledge internalized and that takes time. Time is the medium through which the power of Jesus Christ is made manifest in our lives.

I don't remember a day when I didn't know Spanish and then a day when I did. It happened gradually. Think about the Pledge of Allegiance. Most Americans can't recall a specific moment when we went from not knowing to knowing. Rather, we learned it because we repeated it over and over for years and somehow that helped us internalize those words. My mother struggled with some dementia at the end of her life. She could not even remember what day it was, but you should have seen her when we took her to a Boy Scout court of honor for a young man receiving his Eagle. When the flag was brought forward and we were asked to recite the Pledge, she did not hesitate for two seconds. The words just flowed out of her because they had become part of her.

Grace is not how we cram for the final judgment. How many of you have crammed for a test? How many have forgotten what you learned the minute the test was over? Grace is not about passing a test. It is about becoming more like Christ and our Heavenly Parents. The final judgment will not be about writing the correct answers on a paper, but having them written on our hearts.

When I was a young man in high school I joined the debate team and on Saturdays we would board a school bus and go to various competitions throughout the state. At the end of the day we would load up the bus and head for home. To pass the time, my friends and I would play a game called Matthew, Mark, Luke, and John. We sat with our knees facing the aisle and then we slapped our knees, clapped our hands, and clicked our fingers in unison. Each time we clicked our fingers, whoever was "it" had to call out someone else's name or number and then that person had to repeat the process without breaking the rhythm. If you repeated it successfully, you'd move up one seat; if you didn't, you had to go to the back of the bus.

I would get caught up in the excitement of the moment and want to reach the front of the bus without making a mistake. Then inevitably I would mess up and be sent to the back of the bus, where I would spend the next little while complaining, "This game is dumb and anyone who likes this game is dumb!" However, before long I started moving forward again until my brain would freeze and I would end up at the back of the bus. What I know now that I didn't understand then is that, wherever I was on the bus, the bus was still taking me home. Even when I sat at the back, the bus was still moving forward.

Next time you feel like your brain freezes and you get sent to the back of the bus, just stay on! Enduring to the end doesn't mean enduring without errors. It means enduring *despite* errors. It means staying on the bus no matter where we currently sit.

I know it's hard. We say, "I'll never do it again." And then we do it. Then we say, "I swear I will never do it again." Then we do it. Then we say, "For reals—pinky promise—I will never do it again." I actually overheard a Beehive and a Scout having a fight about which is stronger—pinky promise or Scout's honor. I said, "It doesn't matter because you are probably going to break both of them."

So when we break both Scout's honor and pinky promises, and even when we break promises made before God, angels, and witnesses—stay on the bus. Grace is not a prize for the righteous. It is the source of righteousness. Grace is not a reward for the worthy. It is the source of worthiness. Grace is not waiting for us to get our act together, break all our bad habits, and show up at the front of the bus. Grace is the divine help we receive throughout the entire perfecting process. When you don't recognize answers to prayer and you don't recognize tender mercies, open your eyes and you *will* recognize grace shaping your character, changing your heart, and perfecting your soul.

Another favorite song by Kenneth Cope is titled "Tell Me":

> *Tell me, tell of a God that won't slow down*
> *That will not rest till I am found*
> *Tell of His heart that won't let go*
> *His arms that long to hold me.*[6]

I love the song because it describes what I have attempted to do throughout my life—to testify that Heavenly Father and Jesus Christ will not rest until we are found. They will perfect us as we stay in our covenant relationship with them. They will get us home as we stay on the bus.

FIGHTING THE FEAR THAT WE AREN'T GOOD ENOUGH

Kathy E. Zeyer

A few months ago, I was asked to take a survey of the different topics that had been selected for this Brigham Young University Women's Conference. The conference committee was trying to get a feel for which sessions would have the highest attendance. I came across the topic "Fighting the Fear That We Aren't Good Enough." I thought to myself, "I want to go to that one! I never feel good enough . . ." To my surprise, I ended up receiving the assignment to speak on the subject!

As I pondered this topic, I reflected back to when I was a young Primary girl, working to memorize the Articles of Faith. I remember thinking, "Wow! The thirteenth Article of Faith is the longest. This is going to be really hard." In pondering that scripture, I think at times we worry that we are falling short of "being honest, true, chaste, benevolent, virtuous, and . . . doing good to all men." We should "believe all things, . . . hope all things, . . . [endure] many things, and hope to be able to endure all things." We should also, in our spare time, be seeking after all that is "virtuous, lovely, or of good report or praiseworthy." My old Primary self was right—that is hard!

As sisters in the Church, I think we particularly fall into the trap of thinking we have to be perfect in doing it all, that if we fall short, we are never going to make it.

J. Devn Cornish of the Seventy talked about the concept of fearing we are not good enough in his talk during October 2016 conference titled, "Am I Good Enough? Will I Make It?" He taught us:

"Let me be direct and clear. The answers to the questions 'Am I good enough?' and 'Will I make it?' are 'Yes! You are going to be good enough' and 'Yes, you are going to make it as long as you keep repenting and do not rationalize or rebel.' The God of heaven is not a heartless referee looking for any excuse to throw us out of the game. He is our perfectly loving Father, who yearns more than anything else to have all of His children come back home and live with Him as families forever. He truly gave His Only Begotten Son that we might not perish but have everlasting life! Please believe, and please take hope and comfort from this eternal truth. Our Heavenly Father intends for us to make it! That is His work and His glory."[1]

Oftentimes, as sisters in the Church, as we navigate life and strive to do our best, we sometimes struggle a bit with what I would term "Productive Self-Assessment" versus "Nonproductive Self-Assessment."

That is where I would like to focus my remarks today.

I'd like to talk first about the type of self-assessment that is nonproductive. Satan has some cunning tools that he uses that can make us feel hopeless, and therefore keep us from progressing.

Discouragement, envy, jealousy, self-loathing, low self-esteem, low confidence, negative self-talk, comparing ourselves to others, competing, or poor self-image. These things can keep us feeling discouraged and despondent and keep us from seeing and reaching our potential.

Elder Cornish mentioned in his talk:

"Our members often ask, 'Am I good enough as a person?' or 'Will I really make it to the celestial kingdom?' Of course, there is no such thing as 'being good enough.' None of us could ever 'earn' or 'deserve' our salvation, but it is normal to wonder if we are acceptable before the Lord, which is how I understand these questions.

"Sometimes when we attend church, we become discouraged even by sincere invitations to improve ourselves. We think silently, 'I can't do all these things' or 'I will never be as good as all these people.' . . .

"Please, my beloved brothers and sisters, we must stop comparing ourselves to others. We torture ourselves needlessly by competing and comparing. We falsely judge our self-worth by the *things* we do or don't have, and by the *opinions of others*. If we must compare, let us compare how we were in the past to how we are today and even to how we want to be in the future. The only opinion of us that matters is what our Heavenly Father thinks of us. Please sincerely ask Him what He thinks of you. He will love and correct but never discourage us; that is Satan's trick."[2]

Sometimes I think we look all around us and compare our own lives to other peoples' seemingly ideal situations. In a recent talk by Brother Hank Smith, an assistant professor at BYU, he mentioned how social media plays into this misconception. He talked about the fact that people, for the most part, tend to post on social media the outwardly best parts of their lives: the nice vacations, the perfectly dressed children, the loving spouse. He mentioned that sometimes the reality is something like having a mostly perfectly cleaned house, but when people come over you shut the door to your messy laundry room.

We then look at those around us and think for instance, "Wow, look at Susie. She's got it all together. She's always in high-profile callings in the Church. She's always dressed in the nicest clothes. She's prettier than I am, skinnier, and she has the perfect house, nicer cars, well-behaved children, and wonderful husband." We look at other peoples' trips to Hawaii, and our big trip for the year was to the pond down the street. We can make ourselves crazy comparing our situations to others.

The fact is we often don't know what people are really struggling with, or what is just outside the photo or illusion of perfection.

Comparing and competing are two things that can create discouragement, envy, and jealousy, all which keep us from appreciating our own blessings, and can keep us from seeing our own potential. We need to see ourselves as the Savior does and keep our focus on those things that are of eternal significance.

I have a dear sister-in-law who, years ago, was pregnant with her second child and was experiencing horrible morning sickness. She had been particularly ill one morning when she was alone at home with her two-year-old daughter. That daughter decided she wanted to go outside and ran out the door and down the street. I should mention this sweet little girl had just taken off all of her clothes, had picked up a screwdriver, and was running as fast as she could go. Not the safest situation. This poor sister-in-law in her morning-sick state went running after her, in her bathrobe, unshowered, probably with dried throw-up on her chin. When she finally caught up with her little track star and turned for home, she saw two sisters from her ward coming by with their children in their strollers. Of course, they looked like they had just come from the beauty parlor, and their perfect children were dressed immaculately in their cute clothes, riding in their nice clean strollers. It was one of those moments of great timing where I am sure my sister-in-law wanted to crawl under a rock and hide.

The point is—are we running down the street of our life in our bathrobe, looking at others around us who seem to have it all together, and comparing ourselves, seeing our current situation as somehow less than the ideal?

We as women often compare ourselves with others, particularly in ways that have no eternal significance, such as outward appearances—clothing, beauty, or earthly possessions. We allow this to distract us from what is important. We become discouraged and thus have feelings that are not conducive to our spiritual progress and eternal potential, or how the Lord truly looks upon us. We should never buy into Satan's message of "I'm never going to be good enough, so why try?" We need to understand that in this life we will never be perfect, but we can strive to be perfect in *trying*.

Neal A. Maxwell, when he was a member of the Seventy, in his 1976 conference address titled, "Notwithstanding My Weakness," taught us the following:

"Some of us who would not chastise a neighbor for his frailties have a field day with our own. Some of us stand before no more harsh a judge than ourselves, a judge who stubbornly refuses to admit much happy evidence and who cares nothing for due process. Fortunately, the Lord loves us more than we love ourselves. A constructive critic truly cares for that which he criticizes, including himself, whereas self-pity is the most condescending form of pity; it soon cannibalizes all other concerns."[3]

When we can learn to focus on our own strengths and blessings, and compare our progress not with others, but with ourselves, we grow closer to our Heavenly Father. We need to look inside and discover things we do that *are* good, progress we *have* made, and goals we *have* achieved.

We need to focus on our *own measuring stick.*

It is wonderful to surround ourselves with those who are great examples, and through their association we can become better people. There is a difference between admiring those around us who have characteristics we want to emulate and becoming discouraged, thinking we will never measure up to what we perceive as their strengths. We need to understand that all of us have our own strengths and weaknesses, and *that* is what makes us all so beautifully diverse.

Elder Jeffrey R. Holland taught in the April 2017 general conference that the fact that we all have diverse talents and challenges is part of Heavenly Father's plan. He compared it to different voices that sing together in a choir. He taught:

"On those days when we feel a little out of tune, a little less than what we think we see or hear in others, I would ask us . . . to remember it is by divine design that not all the voices in God's choir are the same. It takes variety—sopranos and altos, baritones and basses—to make rich music. To borrow a line quoted in the cheery correspondence of two remarkable Latter-day Saint women, 'All God's critters got a place in the choir.' When we disparage our uniqueness or try to conform to fictitious stereotypes—stereotypes driven by an insatiable consumer culture and idealized beyond any possible realization by social media—we lose the richness of tone and timbre that God intended when He created a world of diversity. . . . Believe in yourself, and believe in Him. Don't demean your worth or denigrate your contribution. Above all, don't abandon your role in the chorus. Why? Because you are unique; you are irreplaceable. The loss of even one voice diminishes every other singer in this great mortal choir of ours, including the loss of those who feel they are on the margins of society or the margins of the Church . . . 'Come as you are,' a loving Father says to each of us, but He adds, 'Don't plan to stay as you are.'"[4]

We need to see ourselves and our potential the way our Heavenly Father does. I was recently talking about this subject with my twenty-one-year-old daughter, who I think is beautiful inside and out. She asked me if I had seen an internet video that had been created as part of an ad campaign. It addressed the fact that we are more beautiful than we think we are. Some of you may have seen this. In the video, they asked women to sit on one side of a curtain and a professional sketch artist sat on the other side. The artist asked each woman to describe what they looked like—describing each facial feature, the way *they* think they looked. They also asked each woman to spend some time with another person—a total stranger.

That total stranger then spent time with the sketch artist describing what they thought the person looked like. The artist never saw who he was sketching. They then displayed the two portraits side by side and allowed the women to look at their two sketches. Without fail, the sketch that was created from the description by the total stranger was more attractive than the sketch drawn using their own description, proving that we very often see ourselves in a *more negative light than other people see us*. I know our Heavenly Father sees our potential, our strengths. He recognizes the characteristics about us that are inherently good.

We should strive to see ourselves in that light.

Now that I've talked about some areas of self-assessment that are nonproductive, I'd like to talk about some ways that we can make self-assessment positive and productive.

Taking steps to become more like the Savior, amidst the trials and struggles of life, is what we came here to earth to do. It is a vital part of the plan of salvation. Our loving Heavenly Father loves us and wants us to return to Him and receive every possible blessing.

Through the restored gospel of Jesus Christ, we have the great blessing of inspired leaders that love and teach us, the priceless gift of the scriptures to help us navigate this life, and the chance to have the constant companionship of the Holy Ghost to guide and direct us as we strive to be the best we can be.

In the October 2015 general conference, Larry R. Lawrence of the Seventy gave a talk entitled, "What Lack I Yet?" He counseled:

"If we are humble and teachable, the Holy Ghost will prompt us to improve and lead us home, but we need to ask the Lord for directions along the way."[5]

He spoke of the account in the New Testament about the rich young ruler. This young man was already, in his mind, keeping the Ten Commandments, but inquired of the Savior, "What lack I yet?" The Savior told him to go and sell his possessions to give to the poor. This troubled the young man. It was evidently a weakness of his, and the Savior perceived this.

We need to be humble and teachable enough to sincerely ask our Heavenly Father, "What lack I yet?" And then have the desire and self-discipline to act upon it.

One of my favorite scriptures in the Book of Mormon is

found in the book of Ether, and it teaches us that being aware of our shortcomings is not necessarily a bad thing, but with the Lord's help, we have the potential to make those weaknesses our strengths.

In Ether 12:27 we learn, "And if men [and women] come unto me I will show unto them their weakness. I give unto men weakness that they may be humble; and my grace is sufficient for all men that humble themselves before me; for if they humble themselves before me, and have faith in me, then will I make weak things become strong unto them."

In the book of Alma, when Aaron teaches Lamoni's father, the king asked, "What shall I do that I may have this eternal life of which thou hast spoken? Yea, what shall I do that I may be born of God, . . . and receive His Spirit, that I may be filled with joy?" (Alma 22:15). Lamoni's father then bowed down to the earth and said, "I will give away all my sins to know thee" (v. 18).

Elder Lawrence relates in his talk several examples of brothers and sisters who sincerely inquired of the Lord where they could improve, and what was keeping them from progressing. He relates the account of a faithful mother who asked the question, "What lack I yet?" Elder Lawrence related:

"In her case, the response from the Spirit came immediately: 'Stop complaining.' This answer surprised her; she had never thought of herself as a complainer. However, the message from the Holy Ghost was very clear. In the days that followed, she became conscious of her habit of complaining. Grateful for the prompting to improve, she determined to count her blessings instead of her challenges. Within days, she felt the warm approval of the Spirit."[6]

We all have areas of strengths and weaknesses. When

inquiring of our Heavenly Father for help, while listening to the counsel of our church leaders, or by studying the scriptures, we should listen to the Spirit for promptings of areas where we could improve. This could be more closely observing the Sabbath day, controlling our temper, being more patient with our spouse or our children, cleaning up our language, being a better listener, forgiving someone who has wronged us.

Elder Lawrence went on to say:

"The Holy Ghost doesn't tell us to improve everything at once. If He did, we would become discouraged and give up. The Spirit works with us at our own speed, one step at a time, or as the Lord has taught, 'Line upon line, precept upon precept.'"[7]

During a particularly challenging time for the Prophet Joseph Smith, after the 116 manuscript pages had been lost and he must have been realizing and struggling with his own weaknesses, he received counsel found in Doctrine and Covenants 10:4–5:

"Do not run faster or labor more than you have strength and means provided to enable you to translate; but be diligent until the end. Pray always, that you may come off conqueror; yea, that you may conquer Satan, and that you may escape the hands of the servants of Satan that do uphold his work."

Joseph was counseled to not run faster than he had strength, but to be "diligent until the end" and to "pray always that you may come off conqueror."

In other words, keep trying, and ask for divine help.

One opportunity we have for positive, productive self-assessment is when we partake of the sacrament each week. This is a chance we have to renew our baptismal covenants and reflect on how we are doing in our own progress. I would suggest that during this time, we should not only be looking inward at an area where we could improve during the coming week, but also to recognize any progress we have made, any good we have accomplished during the week. It's important not only to recognize our shortcomings, but to recognize in ourselves the good we have done, or where we have improved.

A recent blog article on LDS.org titled, "You're Not Messing Up God's Plan for You," by Ariel Szuch really resonated with me, and I wanted to share it here. She wrote:

"Following Jesus through the continuous process of exercising faith in Him, repenting, making and keeping covenants, and receiving the gift of the Holy Ghost is the way back to the Father. As long as I continue in that process, I'm following the plan.

"One day recently I was feeling particularly discouraged about my seeming inability to 'get a grip' on my life and measure up to my own expectations. On one side of the whiteboard in my room I wrote down all my expectations for myself. Then I drew a line, and on the other side, across from each of my statements, I wrote what I felt God would have to say about it.

"It all came down to this: Me learning *is* the plan. Me *changing* is the plan. And there are a lot of good ways to do that. My baptism was a commitment to keep learning and keep turning to Christ. It's not a commitment to be perfect (and thus fail as soon as I make my first mistake); it's a commitment to keep practicing. If I keep turning to Jesus after turning away, if I'm committed to keep learning, keep trying, and rest when I need to, I'm following His plan for me."[8]

In Hebrews 10:35–36, the Apostle Paul taught: "Cast not away therefore your confidence, which hath great recompense of reward. For ye have need of patience, that, after ye have done the will of God, ye might receive the promise."

We need to have confidence that we can attain all blessings with the help of our Father in Heaven and through the Atonement of Jesus Christ.

Lastly, I'd like to address the issue of fear—the fear we may not measure up, that we aren't good enough. Fear is a tool of the adversary. It doesn't reflect the loving nature of our Heavenly Father or His plan for us.

We learn in 2 Timothy 1:7, "For God hath not given us the spirit of fear; but of power, and of love, and of a sound mind." This scripture makes reference to the things that have power over fear—blessings that have been bestowed on us such as the power of the gospel, the power of faith and hope, the power of the priesthood, the power of love. These things are all stronger than fear.

At times in my life when I have felt discouraged, or struggled with my own self-worth, I have found great comfort in Isaiah's counsel:

"Fear thou not; for I am with thee: be not dismayed; for I am thy God: I will strengthen thee; yea, I will help thee; yea, I will uphold thee with the right hand of my righteousness" (Isaiah 41:10).

We can't let fear of not measuring up keep us from moving forward. Every day, be the best you can be. One day at a time. Line upon line, precept upon precept. If you fall down, get back up. Keep trying. Your Heavenly Father loves you more than you can comprehend.

I'd like to read a verse from one of my favorite hymns, "I Know That My Redeemer Lives":

> *He lives to grant me rich supply.*
> *He lives to guide me with his eye.*

He lives to comfort me when faint.
He lives to hear my soul's complaint.
He lives to silence all my fears.
He lives to wipe away my tears.
He lives to calm my troubled heart.
He lives all blessings to impart.[9]

I bear testimony of the power of the Atonement of Jesus Christ and for the love that our Heavenly Father and our Elder Brother have for each one of us individually. I know if we pray for help, and keep trying, we can all return to live with them someday and partake of the glorious blessings they have in store for us and that we will then see ourselves as they see us.

SHARING THE
KNOWLEDGE OF
A SAVIOR

Elder Gary E. Stevenson

In May of 2017, Elder Gary E. Stevenson spoke at the 2017 BYU Women's Conference. His address was a multimedia presentation about the great opportunities and also the associated dangers of social media in today's evolving world. The extent of this powerful address cannot fully be captured in written form alone; however, excerpts from Elder Stevenson's address have been included in this compilation. To view the entire address, and share in the multimedia experience with Elder Stevenson, please visit lds.org.[1]

I consider it a great blessing and significant responsibility to have received the assignment to speak at this year's BYU Women's Conference, one which came from the First Presidency nearly nine months ago. I admit that this assignment seems to have created more consternation for me than even a general conference speaking assignment. Partly this stems from hearing reports when I was younger of inspiring Women's Conference messages from my mother, sisters, aunts, and cousins—or in my early married life, from Lesa. And so this afternoon, unbeknownst to them, the bar has been set very high for me, by these very important women in my life.

We are the Church of Jesus Christ, established in the latter-days. In the same way that the Lord instructed His ancient disciples, we have been charged in the latter days to "Go ye into all the world, and preach the gospel to every creature" (Mark 16:15).

The ancient prophet Nephi succinctly and clearly summarized this mission and message, and the object behind it. "And we talk of Christ, we rejoice in Christ, we preach of Christ, we prophesy of Christ, and we write according to our prophecies, that our children may know to what source they may look for a remission of their sins" (2 Nephi 25:26).

In the book of Mosiah, we read about how ancient Book of Mormon prophet King Benjamin gathered his people throughout the land, at the site of the temple, caused a tower to be erected, and taught them.

As he taught them, he also prophesied to them of our day, "And moreover, I say unto you, that the time shall come when the knowledge of a Savior shall spread throughout every nation, kindred, tongue, and people" (Mosiah 3:20).

One of the most precious gifts to treasure within our families and to give to others is "the knowledge of a Savior," or of Jesus Christ.

The opening of the dispensation of the fulness of times in 1820 brought an enlightenment upon all mankind, and a waterfall of technological advancements. It brought with it the industrial age, and communication tools allowing the prophecy of King Benjamin to be fulfilled.

As a member of the Quorum of the Twelve, called as a special witness of the name of Christ in all the world—with specific assignments in both the public affairs and communication services committees, I am able to focus toward the fulfillment of this prophecy—that the knowledge of a savior is spread throughout the world—using the latest technologies available to us.

THROUGHOUT EVERY NATION, KINDRED, TONGUE, AND PEOPLE

Historically, advancements in print and the invention of radio and TV enabled the message of the Restoration to go throughout the world.

We find numerous examples of this, some of which are within our memory. Within ten years of the first vision, 5,000 copies of the Book of Mormon were published, the same month the Church was organized. Since then, over 175 million copies have been printed. On Sunday mornings, you can listen to the over 4,500 broadcasts of *Music and the Spoken Word*, the first of which was broadcast on live radio in 1929. The first broadcast of general conference on TV took place in 1949.

Throughout Every
Nation, Kindred, Tongue, and People

PRINT	RADIO	TV
1830	1929	1949

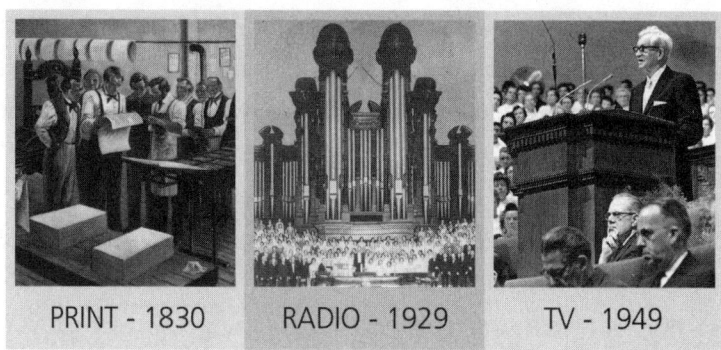

PRINT - 1830   RADIO - 1929   TV - 1949

Interestingly, even in 1966, President David O. McKay began speaking of things to come, things which would spread the knowledge of a Savior throughout every nation, kindred, tongue and people. Here are his prophetic words: "Scientific discoveries that 'stagger the imagination'" would make possible the preaching of the gospel to every kindred, tongue, and people. And further: "Discoveries latent with such potent power, either for the blessing or the destruction of human beings, as to make man's responsibility in controlling them the most gigantic ever placed in human hands. . . . This age is fraught with limitless perils, as well as untold possibilities."[2]

President Spencer W. Kimball described *his* vision in 1974: "I believe that the Lord is anxious to put into our hands inventions of which we laymen have hardly had a glimpse."[3]

With technological advances in communication and media coming largely on the heels of the internet, it seems to me that we have witnessed in our lifetimes the literal fulfillment of the prophecy of King Benjamin, President McKay, and President Kimball.

There is also a clear pattern of the adoption of these technologies to build the Lord's Kingdom on earth. I would like to share examples of this with you.

In 1996, the Church officially began use of the web as a

messaging and communication vehicle. Since then, an estimated 260 Church-sponsored websites have been introduced, including sites available in nearly every country where members of the Church live—in their local language.

I share two familiar examples of these websites. First, LDS .org, established in 1996, which today receives over 24 million new visitors a year, and over 1 million average visitors each week. Many members find curriculum for teaching and past general conference talks here. Second, Mormon.org, a website designed to introduce the gospel to our neighbors and friends who are not members of the Church. This site receives over 16 million unique visitors a year.

Of course, technologies evolve at a breakneck pace, requiring considerable effort and resources to keep up. With the invention of smartphones came the power to harness and access massive amounts of data in a handheld modality.

Much of this data is organized in the form of "mobile applications," or *apps*. The first Church-sponsored app was published in 2007. Examples abound of our beneficial use of mobile apps to spread our knowledge of a Savior to every nation, kindred, tongue, and people. They are being used millions of times a week with millions of users.

Church Mobile Apps

GOSPEL LIBRARY	MORMON CHANNEL	LDS TOOLS	LDS MUSIC	FAMILY TREE
7.5 MILLION USERS	685,000 USERS	2.8 MILLION USERS	1.8 MILLION USERS	1.3 MILLION USERS

Beginning in about 2010, the Church began an earnest adoption of the use of social media to accomplish "spreading the knowledge of a Savior."

This is a very fast-moving and dynamic digital modality almost incomparable in speed of change.

Throughout Every Nation, Kindred, Tongue, and People					
PRINT	RADIO	TV	WEB	MOBILE APP	SOCIAL MEDIA
1830	1929	1949	1996	2007	2010

One observable characteristic of social media is that as soon as one feels acquainted or comfortable with one platform, a newer, bigger, or perceivably cooler or better one emerges.

It also seems that when our millennial children or grandchildren get even a hint that baby boomers are adopting their social media technology, they quickly move to the newest and latest platform.

Now, having just espoused all the virtues of these new technologies, and demonstrated their appropriate use, I think it is also useful to discuss some of the risks associated with them.

We should all be very aware of the time that can be consumed on social media or in the use of mobile apps. The use of social media also carries a risk of reducing face-to-face interaction, which may be stifling the development of the social skills of many young people.

The hazards associated with inappropriate content cannot be understated. This has created an epidemic of pornography addiction in society, and is negatively affecting and victimizing many Church members and families.

Finally, I offer two additional merging risks, which net is cast over virtually everyone, including young women and millennial mothers and wives. I label these two risks as "Idealized Reality" and "Debilitating Comparisons."

This apparently is not just a sign of our times but, measuring these words from Paul, was in times past as well. 2 Corinthians 10:12 warns, "but they measuring themselves . . . , and comparing themselves among themselves, are not wise."

Elder J. Devn Cornish provided timely counsel in October 2016:

"We torture ourselves needlessly by competing and comparing. We falsely judge our self-worth by the *things* we do or don't have and by the *opinions of others*. If we must compare, let us compare how we were in the past to how we are today—and even to how we want to be in the future."[4]

A FAMILY SECRET

Let me share one of our family secrets, found in this family photo taken some years ago, before the advent of social media. Were this taken today, it likely would be posted to a social media site, presenting a family of four lovely, well-behaved boys, color coordinated, enjoying a harmonious family photo opportunity together. Would you like the real story?

I still remember the phone call from Lesa: "Gary, where are you? We're here at the photographer's outdoor studio; we're all ready to shoot. It hasn't been easy getting the boys all dressed, co-ordinated, and ready. Are you nearly here?" Well, I had forgotten, and hadn't left the office yet!

I was half an hour late, and things had not gone so well in

my absence, bordering on chaos. What had happened? Well, my oldest son had been running through the yard and found an apple tree, picked some apples, and had begun throwing them at the other boys. He hit our third son in his back with an apple and made him fall down and so that son started to cry.

Meanwhile, as that was happening, my second oldest son sat down and his pants went up a little bit and the other kids saw that his socks were white athletic socks, not the church socks that Lesa had laid out for him to wear. She asked him, "Why didn't you wear your church socks?" He said, "Well, I don't like them— they're scratchy!"

And while she's talking to him, our two-year-old son Kyle is running through the yard, trips on something, falls down, and bloodies his nose. Now there's blood dripping down onto his white turtleneck shirt and it's completely stained. This is when I showed up.

The only way to salvage the picture was to reverse the

turtleneck—put it on backwards, hiding the bloodstains from the camera.

As it turns out, while Craig was running around and throwing apples, he fell down and got a huge grass stain on his knee. So, in the picture, his arm is strategically placed, covering up the grass stains.

The third son . . . well, we waited for twenty minutes so his eyes were no longer red from crying.

And of course, Kyle's bloodstains are now on the back of his shirt.

Bryan, well, he now has his hands placed strategically over the top of his white athletic socks so that everything matches.

As for me, well, Gary is in the doghouse because it was my late arrival that was the trigger for all of this.

So when you see these beautiful pictures—of our family, anyway—and lament, "Why can't I get things together and be a picture perfect family, like theirs?"

You all know better!

RISKS ASSOCIATED WITH NEW TECHNOLOGIES

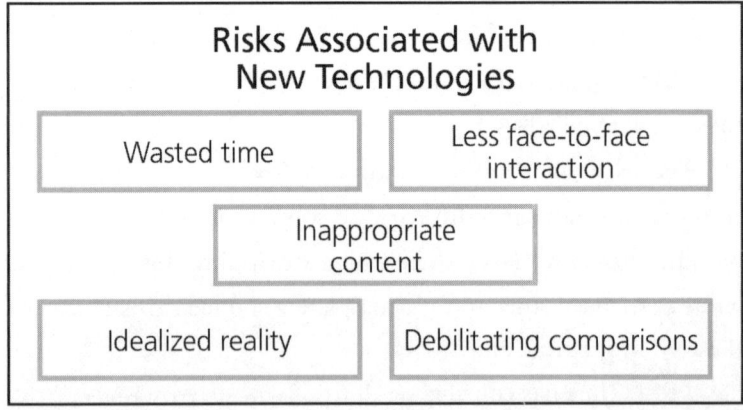

As you can see, we need be mindful of the hazards and risks. Including idealized reality and debilitating comparisons. The world usually is just not as bright as it appears on social media. Nevertheless, there is much good that has, and will, come through these new communication platforms. For example, new instruction was given from the Missionary Department on practical ways social media can be used in missionary work. It is absolutely inspiring to see both the missionaries and members using the many digital resources available to us in an easy, simple, and extremely effective way.

I know that many of you are using technology in appropriate and inspired ways. The benefits of technology will outweigh the associated risks. During a time when I was pondering and praying deeply about this speaking assignment, I woke up very early one morning with a song and its simple lyrics on my mind: "How Lovely Are the Messengers That Preach Us the Gospel of Peace."[5]

Ours is the message of peace, and *you* are lovely messengers that preach it. You can do this through these new and exciting channels of technology. We live in a unique world, in the fulness of times, with the ability to preach the gospel of peace literally at our fingertips.

We have the prophetic words of ancient prophets which perfectly characterize our time and give direction for our day. Again, we read in Mosiah 3:20, "And moreover, I say unto you, that the time shall come when the knowledge of a Savior shall spread throughout every nation, kindred, tongue, and people."

We also have words which come to us through modern-day revelation, speaking to and giving guidance in the use of technology for our time and circumstances. I quote Elder Bednar, "I believe the time has come for us as disciples of Christ to use these inspired tools appropriately and more effectively to testify of God the Eternal Father, His plan of happiness for His children, and His Son, Jesus Christ, as the Savior of the world; to proclaim the reality of the Restoration of the gospel in the latter days; and to accomplish the Lord's work."[6]

I invite each of you to more fully consider your role to preach the gospel of peace as lovely messengers. The best way to do this is one step at a time and in a unique way that works best for you or your family. May each of you have the courage to blog, pin, like, share, post, friend, tweet, snap, and swipe up in a way that will glorify, honor, and respect the will of our loving Heavenly Father and bring a knowledge of the Savior to your family, loved ones, and friends.

NOTES

Eyes to See, Discipline to Create, Glue to Bind—
Converted Unto the Lord

Sharon Eubank

1. "Resurrection did not happen, say quarter of Christians," *BBC News*; available at http://www.bbc.com/news/uk-england-39153121; accessed 14 September 2017.
2. Neal A. Maxwell, BYU fireside, 2 December 1984; audio recording available at speeches.byu.edu; accessed 7 September 2017.
3. See http://www.history.com/this-day-in-history/earthquake-rocks-managua; accessed 7 September 2017.
4. Reyna Aburto, interview with author, 21 April 2017.
5. J. Reuben Clark Jr., in Conference Report, April 1960, 21; paragraphing altered.
6. David A. Bednar, "Converted Unto The Lord," *Ensign*, November 2012, 109.
7. Dieter F. Uchtdorf, "Happiness, Your Heritage," *Ensign*, November 2008, 118, 119.
8. Ibid., 118.
9. M. Russell Ballard, "Mothers and Daughters," *Ensign*, May 2010, 18.
10. Joseph Smith, in *Relief Society Minute Book, Nauvoo, Illinois, Apr. 28, 1842*, Church History Library, 38; punctuation and spelling standardized.
11. Addie Fuhriman, "Singleness: How Relief Society Can Help," *Ensign*, November 1980, 106.
12. Eliza R. Snow, address to Lehi Ward Relief Society, Oct. 27, 1869, Lehi Ward, Alpine (Utah) Stake, in *Relief Society, Minute Book, 1868–79*, Church History Library, Salt Lake City, 26–27.

The Hopeful Keep Moving

Karen J. Ashton

1. William Shakespeare, *Henry V*, in Stanley Wells and Gary Taylor, eds., *The Oxford Shakespeare: The Complete Works, Second Edition* (Oxford: Clarendon Press, 2005), 1.1.1–11, 26–31. Reference is to act, scene, and lines.
2. Henry B. Eyring, *On the Path Home* (Salt Lake City: Deseret Book, 2016), 95.
3. M. Russell Ballard, "The Joy of Hope Fulfilled," *Ensign*, November 1992, 32; emphasis added.
4. Ibid.
5. See Dr. Seuss, *Oh, the Places You'll Go!* (New York: Random House, 1990).
6. Dieter F. Uchtdorf, "The Infinite Power of Hope," *Ensign*, November 2008, 22; paragraphing altered.
7. Uchtdorf, "Perfect Love Casteth Out Fear," *Ensign*, April 2017, 106–7; paragraphing altered.
8. Jeffrey R. Holland, "Tomorrow the Lord Will Do Wonders among You," *Ensign*, May 2016, 126.
9. Neal A. Maxwell, "Encircled in the Arms of His Love," *Ensign*, November 2002, 17.
10. Maxwell, "Hope through the Atonement of Jesus Christ," *Ensign*, November 1998, 62–63; paragraphing altered.
11. Ibid., 63.

How Vast Is Our Purpose

Jean B. Bingham

1. Belle S. Spafford, *A Woman's Reach* (Salt Lake City: Deseret Book, 1974), 21.
2. Emily H. Woodmansee, "As Sisters in Zion," *Hymns of The Church of Jesus Christ of Latter-day Saints* (Salt Lake City: The Church of Jesus Christ of Latter-day Saints, 1985), no. 309; emphasis added.
3. D. Todd Christofferson, "The Moral Force of Women," *Ensign*, November 2013, 29.
4. James E. Faust, "What It Means to Be a Daughter of God," *Ensign*, November 1999, 102.
5. Emma Smith, in *Relief Society Minute Book, Nauvoo, Illinois, 17 March 1842*, 12.
6. Faust, "What It Means to Be a Daughter of God," 100–101.
7. Ibid., 100.
8. *Handbook 2: Administering the Church* (Salt Lake City: The Church of Jesus Christ of Latter-day Saints, 2010), 9.1.1.
9. Woodmansee, "As Sisters in Zion."
10. *Handbook 2*, page 22.
11. Eliza R. Snow, "Female Relief Society," *Deseret News*, 22 April 1868, 81.
12. Dieter F. Uchtdorf, "It Works Wonderfully!" *Ensign*, November 2015, 23.

Living in Grace
Emily Belle Freeman

1. Jeffrey R. Holland, "Songs Sung and Unsung," *Ensign*, May 2017, 51.
2. Dieter F. Uchtdorf, "The Gift of Grace," *Ensign*, May 2015, 110.
3. See Bible Dictionary, s.v. "grace," 697.
4. See *Strong's Exhaustive Concordance: King James Version*, updated edition, s.v. "*charis*," no. G5485 (La Habra, CA: Lockman Foundation, 1995); available at https://www.blueletterbible.org/lang/Lexicon/Lexicon.cfm?strongs=G5485&t =KJV; accessed 7 September 2017.

"Why Do You Stay?"
Barbara Morgan Gardner

1. By the way, I have permission from all of these people to be sharing these stories lest you think I'm just making these up.
2. Eliza R. Snow, "The Lord Is My Trust," *Poems, Religious, Historical, and Political,* vol. 1 (Liverpool: F. D. Richards, 1856), 148, 149.
3. Dieter F. Uchtdorf, "Come Join with Us," *Ensign*, November 2013, 22.
4. David A. Bednar, "Lehi's Dream: Holding Fast to the Rod," *Ensign*, October 2011, 35.
5. Richard G. Scott, "First Things First," *Ensign*, May 2001, 7.
6. Russell M. Nelson, "Drawing the Power of Jesus Christ into Our Lives," *Ensign*, May 2017, 39, 40, 41.
7. Dale G. Renlund, "'That I Might Draw All Men unto Me,'" *Ensign*, May 2016, 39, 40.
8. M. Russell Ballard, "Men and Women in the Work of the Lord," *New Era*, April 2014, 5; paragraphing altered.
9. Nelson, "A Plea to My Sisters," *Ensign*, November 2015, 97.
10. Linda K. Burton, "Is Faith in the Atonement of Jesus Christ Written in Our Hearts?" *Ensign*, November 2012, 112.
11. Bednar, *Increase in Learning* (Salt Lake City: Deseret Book, 2011), 151.
12. Ibid., 154; emphasis added.
13. Scott, "Acquiring Spiritual Knowledge," *Ensign*, November 1993, 86.
14. Bednar, *Increase in Learning*, 156.
15. *Teachings of Presidents of the Church: Joseph Smith* (Salt Lake City: The Church of Jesus Christ of Latter-day Saints, 2007), 49.
16. Jeffrey R. Holland, "Be Not Afraid, Only Believe," address to CES Religious Educators, 6 February 2015; available at https://www.lds.org/broadcasts /article/evening-with-a-general-authority/2015/02/helping-with-the-real -issues?lang=eng; accessed 19 September 2017.
17. See "The Living Christ: The Testimony of the Apostles," *Ensign*, April 2000, 2.
18. Nelson, "Drawing the Power of Jesus Christ into Our Lives," 41.
19. Henry B. Eyring, "'And Thus We See': Helping a Student in a Moment of Doubt," address to CES Religious Educators, 5 February 1993.
20. Gordon B. Hinckley, "CES Evening with a General Authority," February 2000.

21. Thomas S. Monson, "The Power of the Book of Mormon," *Ensign*, May 2017, 86.
22. Nelson, "Drawing the Power of Jesus Christ into Our Lives," 42.
23. Neal A. Maxwell, *Things as They Really Are* (Salt Lake City: Deseret Book, 1980), xii.
24. Nelson, "A Plea to My Sisters," 97.

Becoming a Converted, Covenant-Keeping Woman
Neill F. Marriott

1. *True to the Faith: A Gospel Reference* (Salt Lake City: The Church of Jesus Christ of Latter-day Saints, 2004), 109.
2. Charlotte Elliott, "Just as I Am," *Hymns of Glorious Praise* (Springfield, MO: Gospel Publishing House, 1969), no. 221.
3. Brigham Young, in John A. Widtsoe, ed., *Discourses of Brigham Young* (Salt Lake City: Deseret Book, 1954), 32.
4. Orson F. Whitney, as quoted by Spencer W. Kimball, in *Faith Precedes the Miracle* (Salt Lake City: Bookcraft, 1972), 98.
5. D. Todd Christofferson, "The Blessing of Scripture," *Ensign*, May 2010, 34.
6. Russell M. Nelson, "Drawing the Power of Jesus Christ into Our Lives," *Ensign*, May 2017, 41.
7. Charles Wesley, "A Charge to Keep I Have," *Hymns of Glorious Praise* (Springfield, MO: Gospel Publishing House, 1969), no. 282.

Teaching in the Savior's Way
Camille Fronk Olson

1. David H. Yarn, *J. Reuben Clark: Selected Papers: On Religion, Education, and Youth* (Provo, UT: Brigham Young University Press, 1984), 187.
2. C. S. Lewis, *Mere Christianity* (New York: HarperCollins, 1952), 52.
3. Thomas S. Monson, "Choices," *Ensign*, May 2016, 86.
4. Ezra Taft Benson, "To the Mothers in Zion," address given at a fireside for parents, 22 February 1987; produced as a pamphlet for Church members.
5. *Teachings of Presidents of the Church: Joseph Fielding Smith* (Salt Lake City: The Church of Jesus Christ of Latter-day Saints, 2013), 183–84; Joseph F. Smith taught the same truth this way: "The Spirit of God speaks to our spirits. The Lord does not communicate to us very often through our natural senses, but when He speaks He speaks to the immortal part" (in *Teachings of Presidents of the Church: Joseph F. Smith* [Salt Lake City: The Church of Jesus Christ of Latter-day Saints, 1998], 202–3).

The Test of Life
Bonnie L. Oscarson

1. Neal A. Maxwell, "'Swallowed Up in the Will of the Father,'" *Ensign*, November 1995, 23.
2. Ibid.

3. A. Theodore Tuttle, "The Things That Matter Most," *Ensign*, December 1971, 90.
4. Maxwell, "'Swallowed Up in the Will of the Father,'" 23.
5. Gerald N. Lund, "Answered Prayers," *Friend*, July 2005, 9.
6. Maxwell, "'Swallowed Up in the Will of the Father,'" 23.
7. Brigham Young, quoted in ibid., 24.
8. James E. Faust, "Our Search for Happiness," *Ensign*, October 2000, 5.
9. David A. Bednar, "If Ye Had Known Me," *Ensign*, November 2016, 104.
10. Maxwell, "'Swallowed Up in the Will of the Father,'" 23.
11. Russell M. Nelson, "Drawing the Power of Jesus Christ into Our Lives," *Ensign*, May 2017, 39.
12. Gordon B. Hinckley, "The True Strength of the Church," *Ensign*, July 1973, 48.

The Grandeur of God
Matthew O. Richardson

1. See Helen Bannerman and Fred Marcellino, *The Story of Little Babaji* (New York: Harper Collins, 1996).
2. An illustration of the magic of movies, the battle cruiser model in the film was much larger (more than twice the size) of the seemingly larger Star Destroyer model.
3. See Merriam-Webster's online thesaurus; available at https://www.merriam -webster.com/thesaurus/awesome; accessed 15 September 2017.
4. Harold Kushner, "The Human Soul's Quest for God," *Brigham Young Magazine* (February 1995): 26.
5. Ibid.
6. Cal Newport, *Deep Work: Rules for Focused Success in a Distracted World* (New York: Grand Central Publishing, 2016), 4–7, 182–84, 205–9.
7. Gordon B. Hinckley, "In These Three I Believe," *Ensign*, July 2006, 4.
8. Thomas Groome, *Christian Religious Education: Sharing our Story and Vision* (New York: Jossey-Bass, 1999), 141.
9. Brigham Young, Office Journal, 28 January 1857, Brigham Young Papers, 1801–1877, Church History Library, The Church of Jesus Christ of Latter-day Saints, Salt Lake City, Utah.
10. C. S. Lewis, *The Weight of Glory* (New York: HarperCollins, 1976), 140.

Stay on the Bus
Brad Wilcox

1. See Russell M. Nelson, "Drawing the Power of Jesus Christ into Our Lives," *Ensign*, May 2017, 39–42.
2. Sheri Dew, *Amazed by Grace* (Salt Lake City: Deseret Book, 2015), 4.
3. Dieter F. Uchtdorf, "The Gift of Grace," *Ensign*, May 2015, 107.
4. See Kenneth Cope, "Broken," © 2001 Merge Right Music (BMI); on the music CD *All About You* (Salt Lake City: Shadow Mountain Records, 2008).
5. Charles H. Gabriel, "I Stand All Amazed," *Hymns of The Church of Jesus*

Christ of Latter-day Saints (Salt Lake City: The Church of Jesus Christ of Latter-day Saints, 1985), no. 193.

6. Cope, "Tell Me," *All About You*; used by permission.

Fighting the Fear That We Aren't Good Enough
Kathy E. Zeyer

1. J. Devn Cornish, "Am I Good Enough? Will I Make It?" *Ensign*, November 2016, 33.
2. Ibid., 32–33.
3. Neal A. Maxwell, "Notwithstanding My Weakness," *Ensign*, November 1976, 13.
4. Jeffrey R. Holland, "Songs Sung and Unsung," *Ensign*, May 2017, 49, 50, 51; paragraphing altered.
5. Larry R. Lawrence, "What Lack I Yet?" *Ensign*, November 2015, 33.
6. Ibid., 34.
7. Ibid., 34.
8. Ariel Szuch, "You're Not Messing Up God's Plan for You," blog, 22 February 2017; available at https://www.lds.org/blog/youre-not-messing-up-gods-plan -for-you; accessed 7 September 2017.
9. Samuel Medley, "I Know That My Redeemer Lives," *Hymns of The Church of Jesus Christ of Latter-day Saints* (Salt Lake City: The Church of Jesus Christ of Latter-day Saints, 1985), no. 136.

Sharing the Knowledge of a Savior
Gary E. Stevenson

1. Gary E. Stevenson, "The Knowledge of a Savior"; available at https://www .lds.org/prophets-and-apostles/unto-all-the-world/the-knowledge-of-a-savior ?lang=eng; accessed 19 September 2017.
2. David O. McKay, in Conference Report, October 1966, 4.
3. Spencer W. Kimball, "'When the World Will Be Converted,'" *Ensign*, October 1974, 10.
4. J. Devn Cornish, "Am I Good Enough? Will I Make It?" *Ensign*, November 2016, 33.
5. *Hymns and Songs for the Sunday School* (Philadelphia: Lutheran Publication Society, 1914), no. 267.
6. David A. Bednar, "To Sweep the Earth as with a Flood," Brigham Young University Education Week address, 19 August 2014; available at https:// www.lds.org/prophets-and-apostles/unto-all-the-world/to-sweep-the-earth -as-with-a-flood?lang=eng; accessed 20 September 2017.

CONTRIBUTORS

KAREN J. ASHTON is a wife, mother, and grandmother. She has served as a member of the Young Women general board, and served with her husband, Alan C. Ashton, when he served as president of the Canada Toronto West Mission; they served together as president and matron of the Provo Utah Temple as well. She and Brother Ashton have eleven children. They also founded Thanksgiving Point in Lehi, Utah, as a gift to the community.

JEAN B. BINGHAM was serving as first counselor in the Primary General Presidency when she was called to be the seventeenth General President of the Relief Society in April 2017. She holds a bachelor's and a master's degree in teaching from National Louis University, and taught English as a second language, worked as a volunteer aide in her children's schools, and as a nurse's aide.

She and her husband, Bruce, are the parents of two girls and have been the foster parents of several more children whom they consider part of their family.

SHARON EUBANK is the first counselor in the Relief Society General Presidency and the director of LDS Charities, the humanitarian organization of The Church of Jesus Christ of Latter-day Saints. She holds a bachelor's degree in English from Brigham Young University, and has taught English as a second language in Japan, worked as a legislative aide in the US Senate, owned a retail education store in Provo, Utah, and since 1998, been employed by the LDS Church's Welfare department.

She has served as a full-time missionary in the Finland Helsinki Mission, in ward and stake Sunday School, Relief Society, Young Women, and Primary callings, and as a member of the Relief Society general board.

EMILY BELLE FREEMAN is a best-selling author, popular inspirational speaker, and cofounder of Multiply Goodness. For a few minutes every day she leaves the dishes in the sink and writes about the ever-present goodness of God in the ordinary details of her life.

She has served in the Church as a seminary teacher and Laurel advisor, among other callings. Her greatest joy comes from spending time with her husband, Greg, her five children, and her two grandchildren.

BARBARA MORGAN GARDNER is an assistant professor of Church history and doctrine at Brigham Young University. She completed her bachelor's and master's degree at BYU, her PhD at Utah State University, and did postdoctoral work at Harvard. She worked full time as a teacher, researcher, institute director, and seminary coordinator for Seminaries and Institutes. Formerly the LDS chaplain at Harvard and MIT, she now serves as the LDS chaplain-at-large for higher education. She has served as a stake Young Women president, stake Relief Society counselor, and ward Relief Society president and teacher. She serves on the general Church correlation committee. She is married to Dustin W. Gardner.

NEILL F. MARRIOTT was born and raised in Alexandria, Louisiana, and earned a bachelor's degree in English from Southern Methodist University. At the age of twenty-two, she was converted and baptized into The Church of Jesus Christ of Latter-day Saints, and one year later she married David Marriott in the Salt Lake Temple. They are the parents of eleven children and grandparents of thirty-six. Sister Marriott served with her husband when he was president of the Brazil São Paulo

Interlagos Mission. She was sustained as second counselor in the Young Women General Presidency in April 2013.

CAMILLE FRONK OLSON, professor of ancient scripture, serves as chair of the department of ancient scripture in Religious Education at Brigham Young University. She earned a master's degree and a PhD from BYU. Formerly dean of students at LDS Business College, she has served on the Young Women general board and on the Church's Teacher Development Curriculum Committee. She is a popular speaker and writer whose published books include *Women of the Old Testament; Women of the New Testament; In the Hands of the Potter; Mary, Martha and Me;* and *Too Much to Carry Alone.* She and her husband, Paul, reside in Provo, Utah.

BONNIE L. OSCARSON was called as Young Women General President in April 2013. She attended Brigham Young University and studied commercial art; she returned to BYU after 35 years and earned a bachelor's degree in English. She has served multiple times in both ward and stake Young Women callings, as well as teaching early morning seminary for nine years. She served with her husband, Paul, when he was president of the Sweden Göteborg Mission, and served as the matron when her husband was president of the Stockholm Sweden Temple. She and her husband, Paul, are the parents of seven children and the grandparents of twenty-nine grandchildren.

MATTHEW O. RICHARDSON is the Advancement Vice President of Brigham Young University, having previously taught there as a professor of Church history and doctrine, including serving as associate dean of Religious Education. He holds bachelor's, master's, and EdD degrees from BYU. He and his wife, Lisa, are the parents of four children and grandparents of four grandchildren. He has served as a counselor in the Sunday School General Presidency and serves as a stake president.

ELDER GARY E. STEVENSON was named to the Quorum of the Twelve Apostles on October 3, 2015. He was serving as the presiding bishop of the Church at the time of his call to the Twelve, a position which he had held since April 2012. He was called to the First Quorum of the Seventy in 2008 and served as president of the Asia North Area. His previous Church service includes full-time missionary in the Japan Fukuoka Mission, high councilor, bishop, stake president's counselor, president of the Japan Nagoya Mission, and ward Sunday School teacher. He received a bachelor of science degree from Utah State University.

Elder Stevenson was raised in Cache Valley, Utah. He is married to Lesa Jean Higley, and they are the parents of four sons.

BRAD WILCOX is an associate professor in the department of ancient scripture at Brigham Young University where he also enjoys teaching at Campus Education Week and Especially for Youth. He also loves presenting at Time Out for Women events across the country. He is the author of *The Continuous Atonement, The Continuous Conversion,* and *The 7-Day Christian,* and the BYU devotional, "His Grace Is Sufficient." As a young man, Brad served his mission in Chile and later returned to that country to preside over the Chile Santiago East Mission from 2003 to 2006. He also served as a member of the Sunday School General Board from 2009 to 2014. Brad and his wife, Debi, are the parents of four children and grandparents of five.

KATHY E. ZEYER earned a Bachelor of Science degree in Medical Informatics from Western Governor's University and works as a medical administrator for Revere Health. She has served as president of her ward Relief Society, Young Women, and Primary organizations and as a Gospel Doctrine teacher. She and her husband, Rodney, are the parents of three children.